T0339832

LIGHT RAIL TRANSIT SYSTEMS

LIGHT RAIL TRANSIT SYSTEMS

61 Lessons in Sustainable Urban Development

ROB VAN DER BIJL

NIELS VAN OORT

BERT BUKMAN

ELSEVIER

Elsevier
Radarweg 29, PO Box 211, 1000 AE Amsterdam, Netherlands
The Boulevard, Langford Lane, Kidlington, Oxford OX5 1GB, United Kingdom
50 Hampshire Street, 5th Floor, Cambridge, MA 02139, United States

Notices
Knowledge and best practice in this field are constantly changing. As new research and experience broaden our understanding, changes in research methods, professional practices, or medical treatment may become necessary.

Practitioners and researchers must always rely on their own experience and knowledge in evaluating and using any information, methods, compounds, or experiments described herein. In using such information or methods they should be mindful of their own safety and the safety of others, including parties for whom they have a professional responsibility.

To the fullest extent of the law, neither the Publisher nor the authors, contributors, or editors, assume any liability for any injury and/or damage to persons or property as a matter of products liability, negligence or otherwise, or from any use or operation of any methods, products, instructions, or ideas contained in the material herein.

Library of Congress Cataloging-in-Publication Data
A catalog record for this book is available from the Library of Congress

British Library Cataloguing-in-Publication Data
A catalogue record for this book is available from the British Library

ISBN: 978-0-12-814784-9

For information on all Elsevier publications visit our
website at https://www.elsevier.com/books-and-journals

  Working together
to grow libraries in
Book Aid
International developing countries

www.elsevier.com • www.bookaid.org

Publisher: Joe Hayton
Acquisition Editor: Brian Romer
Editorial Project Manager: Katerina Zaliva
Production Project Manager: Priya Kumaraguruparan
Cover Designer: Vicky Pearson Esser

The front cover image shows an Urbos 3 tram manufactured by the Spanish firm CAF for Kaohsiung (Taiwan). There are no overhead wires since the CAF-developed '*Acumulador de Carga Rapida*' (ACR) system allows vehicles running without it.

The project for this new tramway represents one of our Asian cases. Moreover it is an excellent example of transit oriented development (TOD). The LRV is passing through the spectacular renewed waterfront area. The tower building on the background is a true landmark. It has the shape of the Chinese character 'kaoh' (高) which means 'tall'. In combination with another character (雄), 'mighty', it explains the meaning of Kaohsiung: tall and mighty - 高雄

Typeset by TNQ Technologies

CONTENTS

LIST OF BOXES

Chapter 7

ABOUT THE AUTHORS

Rob van der Bijl is an engineer and urban planner. He received his PhD from the Delft University of Technology, the Netherlands. For many years he has run an independent urban planning office in Amsterdam, the Netherlands. His practice is known for its innovative approach to research and design. He has worked worldwide on many mobility-related projects and transit-oriented developments. All his work is characterized by a multidisciplinary approach to the intersections of urban planning, transport, culture and technology. Moreover, he is visiting professor for 'mobility and space' at Ghent University, Belgium. He has published extensively in journals and books. www.lightrail.nl, www.favas.net.

Niels van Oort is a civil engineer. He received his PhD from the Delft University of Technology, the Netherlands, where he currently works as an

Assistant Professor in the Smart Public Transport Lab. Moreover, he is a public transport consultant at Goudappel Coffeng, with expertise in public transport planning and service reliability, the wider benefits of public transport, and data-driven public transport design. He has contributed to the planning and implementation of several public transport projects in the Netherlands, developed new models for predicting public transport ridership and performance, and published extensively in academic journals and magazines. Find his publications at https://nielsvanoort.weblog.tudelft.nl/.

Bert Bukman is a historian and journalist. For many years he was Editor-in-Chief of Blauwe Kamer, the premier Dutch magazine on landscape architecture, urban planning and urban design. He has published several books and worked on many editorial projects. His motto for corporate communication and public affairs is: 'a good story makes everything possible'.

PREFACE BY PROFESSOR GRAHAM CURRIE

In 2007, humanity passed a threshold we shall never return from; more humans live in cities than don't. From that time humanity is the city, and with it comes the need to make cities liveable nurturing places for the children, friends, and partners we love. Transport remains one of the most significant challenges to urban liveability as the rate of global urbanization increases, traffic congestion, emissions and the imposition of transport infrastructure on cities threaten the quality of the urban fabric which is our home.

In response to these challenges there is a quiet revolution occurring in cities on planet earth. That revolution is public transport. No other mode of travel can cater for high volumes of travellers over such distances in such a space-effective manner with such low emission rates per user. Good public transport is also city shaping so it is no surprise to find the world's most effective, successful and liveable cities are formed around a successful public transport network.

Light rail transit systems represent some of the most appealing aspects of liveable public transport and are the link between light rail and urban development which represents one of the most fascinating opportunities for the future of humanity in cities. It is this link which is at the core of this book, which is a truly international exploration of light rail and the metropolis, using 61 separate cases. A city-oriented perspective of light rail is essential since too often rail projects are viewed from the limited confines of a transport engineering, accounting or a rational economic perspective.

It is becoming increasingly apparent that light rail, and public transport in general, should no longer be viewed as only a transport solution. It is their capacity to change cities, to create sustainable, more effective and liveable communities that justifies the investments which light rail systems require.

This book is well framed to tackle the diversity of topics necessary to explore how light rail and cities can interact. Firstly its international perspective is important since it is the diversity of applications and outcomes which better informs understanding of what is a complex and diverse world. It says much about the resilience of light rail solutions that they can be effective in diverse cases and this is reflected in the 61 cases explored. Chapter 2 considers definitions, which is a necessary and a necessarily evolving topic. Despite a lifetime of experience of developing and planning light rail on five continents, I am constantly surprised by new and unexpected applications of light rail technologies in practice; light rail is not one thing, it's many. Despite often pedantic attempts to describe the diversity of light rail, new approaches abound as humanity adapts technologies to new contexts, even creating light rail systems which are neither light nor, in some cases, rail. Light rail to my mind is a classic case of the 'horses for courses' mantra, we need solutions for cities with a diversity of problems, it's no surprise that a diversity of solutions is therefore needed. Light rail should not be a one-size-fits-all machine; it's is a diverse toolkit applied in diverse ways to meet the diverse challenges of a diverse world. It is therefore, 'diverse' and hence difficult to define. Importantly, Chapter 2 tackles light rail definitions from the city perspective since it is city and not transport only solutions which it seeks to solve.

Chapter 3 considers both new transit-oriented development cases and the important corollary of the transit orientation of existing development and how this relates to light rail in international cases. The excellent advances in Europe, led by many innovations in France are covered but are also placed within a wider international context since good practices are being shared and applied by experienced planners and developers on a global scale. It is books like this which help us better understand these advances and apply them in new projects.

Chapter 4 appropriately explores approaches to justifying light rail investment from the city development context. If it is developmental, environmental and liveability benefits which outweigh conventional travel time benefits in the economic appraisal of light rail projects, what are they? How can they best be achieved and optimised?

Chapter 5 considers tactical issues of quality of service reliability, a major concern for improved ridership and user satisfaction in light rail. Strategic development and management of light rail needs to understand tactical performance implications of design and the operational approaches to improve outcomes for users. Reliability is also the focus of Chapter 6, where the wider impacts of poor performance are illustrated. An evaluation approach is then adopted to show the approaches to improve performance and the benefits to society of achieving this. Chapter 7 explores large light rail project development and implementation experience in many contexts. Factors influencing risk and failure are synthesized and a framework for better project implementation suggested. Chapter 8 concludes the book, summarizing light rail project success factors, and addresses the question of why light rail? An inclusive approach to the implementation of Smart Cities is justified and supported.

As human life on planet earth is increasingly an urban domain, integrated inclusive solutions like light rail are needed to enhance urban development quality and the social, economic performance of our cities into the 21st century. This book provides helpful examples and guidelines to plan and design light rail in such a way that it supports this development and proves to be an important handbook for both urban planners and transport engineers.

Professor Graham Currie PhD
Director, Public Transport Research Group,
Monash University, Australia
Chair, Light Rail Transit Systems Committee,
Transportation Research Board, United States

Tramways in Melbourne occasionally meet state-of-the-art light rail standards. Nevertheless, Australia encounters a true revival of urban rail as our cases in Sydney and Queensland prove. *(Image by Roel Schoemaker.)*

PREFACE BY CEO ROGER VAN BOXTEL

As Professor Graham Currie wrote in his Preface, the last decade has seen the tipping point at which more people now live in cities than outside them. Urbanization is continuing every day. Two thirds of the world's population will be living in cities by 2050. As a result, the pressure on the limited available space and on the climate, air quality, liveability and social cohesion will continue to increase. This creates numerous challenges that also affect our mobility. One of them is a modal shift from car to public transport which is necessary in densely populated areas.

Light rail is one of the solutions for providing the transport that the residents need and it can improve the liveability of cities. Light rail is not, however, a standalone solution, and will always be part of a broader system of mobility that includes other modes of transport. It is therefore not an objective in its own right but one of the solutions for broader issues. Light rail can be a valuable addition in the rich tapestry of a door-to-door journey that comprises multiple modalities. The options are not the same in all countries. Bicycles are often an essential part of the journey in the Netherlands, which is continued by light rail with the passenger subsequently changing to an Intercity train and finally using a shared public transport bicycle for the last mile. And we link that journey together at attractive stations with excellent retail facilities and with offices or homes at the station or close by.

In order to know when and where light rail adds value in this chain, we need to study the entire chain. This includes looking beyond public transport alone: other forms of transport are relevant as well. If you wish, you can use a different modality in the above-mentioned journey, for instance your own car or a shared car. I do not see those as competing with public transport and I am not at all opposed to them — provided they are zero-emission! A broader view is indispensable for solutions to major social problems. We must also look more emphatically at spatial planning and at the complementary mobility policy. In a small country such as the Netherlands, the cohesion of the entire Dutch network is important. We call that 'Network Netherlands'. That network has to help solve larger social, ecological, economic and spatial issues. Light rail most certainly has a role to play here.

These considerations can only be dealt with properly if there is a clear definition of what we are talking about, along with an understanding of the pros and cons of various technologies and approaches. This book fills that gap. It gives a useful factual summary of what light rail is, what it is good at, what went well in the various projects and what we can learn from them. That is extremely valuable for the discussion in The Netherlands and probably elsewhere in the world.

Please allow me to end with the definition. I see 'light rail' as a metaphor: transporting passengers comfortably, well and affordably (including commercial operation and maintenance), quickly and at high frequencies in a fine-meshed network, from the surrounding places up to or sometimes right into the centre of the nearby city. The technology used matters much less to me. Light rail can be a metro, a tram, or even a light regional train. But more important than the means used is that we make a joint effort to enable public transport to make a substantial contribution to higher objectives, such as climate targets. Good analyses are at the heart of that. This book helps the discussion and enriches it. I would therefore like to thank the authors very much for writing it.

Roger van Boxtel
CEO of Dutch Railways, Utrecht, The Netherlands

SUMMARY

In Chapter 1, the story of our Athens case is used to introduce our comprehensive and city-oriented view on light rail. Moreover, all our 61 light rail cases are presented briefly. Finally, we offer a view on a small project in the Caribbean.

In Chapter 2, we discuss definitions of light rail and propose a new improved definition, taking into account the urban characteristics of light rail and contrary to the traditional engineering-driven featuring of light rail. In a dedicated box-section we present cutting-edge examples in an overview of light rail systems (with many images and including information on urban trains, commuter rail, and bus rapid transit).

In Chapter 3, we present an historic overview of urban rail (predecessor of light rail) with the cases of Portland and Los Angeles, focused on 'transit oriented development'. In other words, we explain how and why urban rail in the past and light rail in the present create and structure cities and metropolitan areas. Finally, we return to Europe, to discuss this subject again and make a comparison in this regard between cases in Utrecht (the Netherlands) and Manchester (the UK).

In Chapter 4, we introduce and explain our argumentation of why it's important to invest in the city. Five themes carry the argumentation for light rail in cities: (1) effective mobility, (2) efficient city, (3) economy, (4) environment, and (5) equity. Additionally, we present four principles that elaborate on the environmental theme.

In Chapter 5, we discuss the improved quality of mobility due to light rail (in contrast to bus operations). The 'rail bonus' is explained and the importance of reliability is proved and calculated. The showcase 'Rand-stadRail' in the Netherlands is our base case here.

In Chapter 6, we continue to discuss the importance of reliability (as a clear asset of light rail, in contrast to the bus—using a German case in the city of Aachen) and focus on ways to calculate reliability in improved cost—benefit analyses. Our base case here is the Uithoflijn light rail project in Utrecht, the Netherlands.

In Chapter 7, we start with an overview of incremental light rail planning, with various illustrations from our cases such as in Spain (Vélez-Málaga and Jaén) and Israel (Jerusalem). Secondly, our case study of the RegioTram in Groningen (the Netherlands) is extensively discussed and scrutinized on the bases of in-depth fieldwork. The case of Valenciennes (France) and the alternative bus project of Groningen are used as references. The eventually successful tramway project of Olsztyn (Poland) is staged here as a 'mirror-case' since it allowed us a better understanding of the tragic planning and tender process in Groningen.

Finally, our innovative view on reasons for failures and risks regarding light rail projects are presented in this chapter. A box-section entails 11 cases that demonstrate our international investigation into ways of tendering and contracting light rail projects.

In this last chapter we round up our stories and argumentations. An answer on the question 'why light rail?' is offered, including ways one should assess light rail projects. And we return to all of our 61 cases that are reviewed again. Finally, in this final chapter, our main conclusions are presented and linked to the concept of the 'Smart City'.

CREDITS

The case of Athens in Chapter 1 is based on an interview with Martin Knuijt, by authors Rob van der Bijl and Bert Bukman, published in *Blauwe Kamer* (2014), the premier Dutch magazine on landscape architecture, urban planning, and urban design.

The section in Chapter 2 on the rail circle and associated typology is based on a joint project (2010) by author Rob van der Bijl in collaboration with Jan Baartman and Maurits van Witsen.

The box in Chapter 3 on the light rail project in Edmonton is compiled in collaboration with Axel Kuehn.

The case Zwolle-Kampen in Chapter 4 is based on a project under the auspices of Lightrail.nl (2006—10) by author Rob van der Bijl in collaboration with Maurits van Witsen and Lieuwe Zigterman.

Tim Bunschoten contributed to the rail bonus section in Chapter 5. The interview with tram driver Kees Pronk in the same chapter is compiled in collaboration with Renée van der Bijl.

Author Niels van Oort wrote various articles with Rob van Nes (2004—12) and Robert van Leusden (2014—15) that supported parts of Chapters 5 and 6.

The box in Chapter 7 on the bus project in Groningen is compiled in collaboration with Erwin Stoker and the *OV Bureau Groningen Drenthe* (2014—18).

Translations were done by Annemiek Verhoeven and the authors.

We are grateful to Roger van Boxtel and Graham Currie for their inspiring prefaces.

Special thanks to Emile Jutten of the Dutch Railways for his review and discussions.

All images are made by author Rob van der Bijl, except the images by: L.J.P. Albers, ARCADIS/Team V, André Buikhuizen/*Provincie Groningen*, Martin Glastra van Loon, Bas Govers, Jkan997, JULIANISME, Axel Kuehn, Martin Knuijt/OKRA, METRO/Portland (Oregon), MOs810, Jaap van der Noordt, Oleknutlee, Tom Page, Kees Pronk, Patrick Ruiter/*OV Bureau Groningen Drenthe*, Roel Schoemaker, Smidswater.

Special thanks to Kees Pronk for his contribution to the final compilation of all images in this book.

Special thanks to Raymond Huisman and Arthur Scheltes for multiple visualizations throughout the book.

The three images of the project 'Rethink Athens' in Chapter 1 are made and licensed by OKRA. 'Rethink Athens' is designed by OKRA Landscape Architects, Utrecht, Netherlands.

The image of JULIANISME 'A tram arrived at Zhuhai No.1 High School Station' in Chapter 3 (at page 78) is licensed under a CC BY-SA 4.0 licence. Go to https://creativecommons.org/licenses/by-sa/4.0/ for the full licence text.

The image of Tom Page 'Greater Manchester's Metrolink tram number 3009A, in Salford Quays, Greater Manchester, England' in Chapter 3 (at page 82) is licensed under the Creative Commons Attribution-Share Alike 2.0 Generic license.

The image in Chapter 3 by ARCADIS/Team V of future *RandstadRail Station Lansingerland-Zoetermeer* is licensed by *Gemeente Zoetermeer*/Dennis Dierikx. Project designer: ARCADIS/Team V; project commissioner: *Gemeente Zoetermeer*, Netherlands.

The image in Chapter 3 by Oleknutlee of preserved PE car 1001, is in the public domain.

The aerial view image of the Pearl District by a drone camera in Chapter 3 was made and licensed by Martin Glastra van Loon (Portland, Oregon, US, December 2017) and was specially requested by the author Rob van der Bijl.

Metro's 2040 Growth Concept Map (version September 2014) in Chapter 4 is licensed by Portland Metro/Karen Scott Lowthian (Portland, Oregon, US, February 1, 2018).

The 5E graph in Chapter 4 is owned and licensed by authors Rob van der Bijl and Niels van Oort.

The two graphs on 'Usability' in Chapter 4 are licensed by author Niels van Oort (Goudappel Coffeng).

All figures in Chapters 5 and 6 were compiled and licensed by author Niels van Oort.

The image of MOs810 'Tramway Olsztyn' in Chapter 7 (at page 180) is licensed under the Creative Commons Attribution-Share Alike 4.0 International licence. Go to https://creativecommons.org/licenses/by-sa/4.0/deed.en for the full licence text.

The image of Jkan997 'Map of the Olsztyn tramway network' in Chapter 7 (at page 180) is licensed under the Creative Commons

Attribution-Share Alike 3.0 Unported licence. Go to https://creativecommons.org/licenses/by-sa/3.0/legalcode for the full licence text.

The authors' research for this book has been supported by various institutions — in the Netherlands by the Smart Public Transport Lab of Delft University of Technology, Goudappel Coffeng consultancy, RVDB UrbanPlanning/Lightrail.nl, Favas.net, province of Groningen, project office *Uithof line*, metropolitan region *Rotterdam Den Haag*, magazine *Blauwe Kamer*, and knowledge network *Railforum* — in France by the European Metropolitan Transport Authorities (EMTA) and the EU Interreg-project Sintropher — and in the USA by Transportation Research Board's standing committee on light rail transit (AP075).

CHAPTER 1

Light Rail in Bird's Eye View

The masterplan provides a new green design for the centre along Panepistimiou boulevard in Athens (Greece). *(Image by OKRA.)*

Light Rail Transit Systems
ISBN 978-0-12-814784-9
https://doi.org/10.1016/B978-0-12-814784-9.00001-3

'We've made a magic plan'. That was the headline of an interview with landscape architect Martin Knuijt in a Dutch magazine for landscape architecture and urban planning in the autumn of 2014. In the article, Knuijt, a designer of the Dutch office for landscape architecture OKRA, explained how the *Rethink Athens* project was established.

Rethink Athens is a plan for the redevelopment of the centre of the Greek capital. 'The problems in Athens are clear: too much empty offices, too much traffic, too little urban green and not enough coherent public space', Knuijt sums up in the interview. 'These are the problems all big cities are facing. In Rotterdam, London and elsewhere we've found solutions that we think would be perfect for Athens'.

To the surprise of many, the OKRA plan was selected from more than 70 submissions, including those of renowned international offices. But when you take a closer look, the selection of the OKRA plan is actually quite understandable. It provides a new green design for the centre of Athens, an area of over 50 hectares. The plan offers a solution for the traffic jam on the busy Panepistimiou Boulevard and on two famous squares. The first is the faded Omonia Square with its shutters, junks and graffiti, and the second is the Syntagma Square, which is widely known by television viewers because of the numerous protests against the European Union.

Revolutionary to the OKRA plan is the collection of water in specially constructed underground reservoirs. In the rainy Greek winter, more than 14 million litres of water are collected in pools. This rainwater is used in the summer to water the new urban green, to create a better public realm and to lower the ambient temperature by up to 3°C.

Improved accessibility is a second part of the plan. The driving force is an extension of the existing tramway further into the city, which greatly improves local public transport. The promenade will remain without disturbing overhead lines, because the distance between the two squares can be bridged with batteries. In addition, there is room for pedestrians, cyclists and supply.

Thus, accessibility of the area is greatly improved. Staying on the streets is more enjoyable, because there is a mix of trees that need relatively little water and provide a lot of shade, plus a planting layer with aromatic shrubs that bloom in different seasons.

The third part of *Rethink Athens* relates to the use of the city and its public spaces. Athens must become a vibrant city, which the OKRA team hopes to achieve through a sociocultural programme in the many empty buildings in the area. This will eventually improve the quality of the facilities for artists and entrepreneurs, also in the evening. Artists and start-up companies can use abandoned offices at low cost, and in vacant stores there is room for pop-up theatres, restaurants and stores.

In effect, the Okra plan for the redevelopment of Athens is a plan that indicates a new dimension in thinking about the city. If we continue with urbanization in the current way — too many cars, serious decay; too little structure, too little green — many metropolitan areas run the risk of becoming unlivable. Something has to be done, and *Rethink Athens* gives a new, useful direction. It offers a perspective on the necessary investments in the city for the coming decades.

Why do we focus so extensively on this plan at the beginning of a book on light rail? Because *Rethink Athens's* carrier is the tram project. Without the tram, no underground water basins, no urban green, no improved accommodation quality and thus no improved economic conditions would result from this. Without the tram project, the centre of Athens would remain the prelude to hell that it is now, according to some observers.

This book is therefore a plea for investing in the city with light rail. In particular, lessons are learned from projects in European cities with their long tram histories and many recent light rail projects elsewhere. In particular, our three main cases, the Dutch projects *RandstadRail* (Rotterdam/The Hague), *Uithof line* (Utrecht) and *RegioTram* (Groningen) are used to draw lessons on what went well and what didn't.

It is clear to us and many others that the importance of urban accessibility is greater than ever, and the role of light rail cannot be overestimated. This applies to cities worldwide. Light rail is much more than transport: light rail also means a social impulse, economic growth opportunities, a better environment, greater attractiveness and more favourable conditions in general.

The new tramway in Oranjestad (Aruba) under construction in upgraded public realm of downtown (situation in January 2013). *(Image by Kees Pronk.)*

The importance of light rail is also illustrated by the small tram project *Arutram* in Oranjestad on the island of Aruba in the Caribbean. This project has similar characteristics to *Rethink Athens* in Greece. It has the same three objectives, namely a better environment, improved accessibility and a livable city. But where *Rethink Athens* for the time being only exists on paper, *Arutram* has been implemented (opened in February 2013).

The line (2.7 km) connects the cruise terminal and the city centre, but it is more than a short, mainly tourist tramway. It is part of the revitalization of the city centre. By improving accessibility, tourists are expected to spread more widely over the island, and stores will profit from it. With the refurbishment of public space, the realization of a new pedestrian zone and the strengthening of urban greenery, the tramway is intended to increase the quality of life. The project represents a strong green orientation of Aruba. For example, batteries augmented by hydrogen fuel power the trams.

Unfortunately, in the 61 cases highlighted in this book, success and light rail do not always come together. At all stages of a project, it may fail: during the preparation, during the tendering, during construction and even after opening. In our case study of the Groningen *RegioTram* project, all relevant factors that ultimately led to its failure (such as transport, urban planning, governance, politics, organization) are discussed. The project is considered an important international lesson and reference for current and future urban infrastructure projects.

The more successful Dutch projects *RandstadRail* and *Uithof line* have also been subject to intensive research. Particular attention is paid to the economic, social and environmental importance of urban tram projects. What is the added value of a tram compared with other non-rail public transport modalities? This question is relevant for a good understanding of the projects, and is also relevant because, in the opinion of the authors, the benefits of tram (e.g., vs. bus) are insufficiently considered in the societal cost–benefit analyses. In addition, 58 other cases are discussed which reinforce and confirm the conclusions of the three above-mentioned projects.

This book is divided into eight chapters, in which more detailed topics are discussed. In Chapter 2, light rail is raised as a public asset worth investing in. However, for a better understanding of the value of light rail for a city, a more precise definition is required than the current 'container concept'. Light rail has its own characteristics, as shown in this chapter. The most characteristic feature of a light rail vehicle is its ability to mix with other traffic, in functional and legal terms. This has a major influence on the vehicle's characteristics.

Take the example of a situation in the city operated by light rail, for example a shopping mall with adjacent facilities plus housing. In this case, the tramway is usually in the public realm, so there are grade intersections and in some parts the tram shares the space with the remaining traffic, and even with pedestrians. In this situation, there are about two or three stops, fully integrated in public space, and thus connected to the area via relatively short walkways on ground level, with no height differences.

In exactly the same situation, but then served by metro or regional train, only one station would suffice, most likely underground or elevated by an embankment or viaduct. Integration with the area is not necessarily worse, but certainly different. In any event, public transport is less visible. But, more importantly, the walking distances are greater and more difficult, because to get to or from the station, height differences must be overcome.

Chapter 3 states that since the late 1970s, after decades of demolition, rail infrastructure has expanded considerably in many European countries. The Dutch New Town Zoetermeer got a regional train connection with The Hague, which was used locally to access the new neighbourhoods of the new town by means of a relatively large number of stations. In the Rotterdam area, at that time, the metro was expanded along the route of a former regional tramway, towards the new towns of Hoogvliet and, eventually, Spijkenisse. The Schiphol airport line was also opened and the new town Almere received a train connection with Amsterdam in the late 1980s.

Similar developments have been seen in other Western countries. This renewed orientation of urban development on high-quality public transport is part of a stormy urban development in the same period. It is therefore not surprising that the concept of transit oriented development (TOD) was subject to increasing interest.

Chapter 4 states that investments in public facilities can be justified on the basis of various considerations. This also applies to light rail projects. Five areas of argument appear to be essential for light rail. They are described in this chapter as: (1) effective mobility, (2) efficient city, (3) economy, (4) environment and (5) equity. Additionally we present four principles that elaborate the environmental theme.

'Effective mobility' has to do with proper operation. Given a certain transport value, the operation will have to be profitable to a certain extent. An 'efficient city' has to do with the extent to which light rail contributes to the quality of urban design/planning and traffic design/planning. 'Economy' indicates the indirect and direct economic effects of light rail, such as changed values of land and real estate. 'Environment' summarizes the performance of light rail in relation to sustainable development. The less unambiguous concept of 'equity' ultimately relates to the role of light rail as a public supply that brings about desired social changes. This appears to play a role in many light rail projects.

As stated in Chapter 5 Light rail has the potential to make a leap in the quality of public transport for users. Experts discuss higher frequencies and improved comfort by new vehicles and the upgrading of stops. Due to an increased number of stops (compared to former or alternative heavy rail train services), the required travel time from 'door to door' is decreased, while the overall travel time remains the same.

Reliability is a very important quality aspect in public transport, both for travellers and for carriers. However, a good (quantitative) substantiation of such claims is scarce. This chapter provides support for quantitative research. Light rail does indeed have this potential, if it is well designed. Evidence is obtained from research for our Dutch case *RandstadRail* (focussing on The Hague–Zoetermeer connection).

In order to ensure that the investments are properly compared with the benefits, an appropriate assessment framework is necessary, as argued in Chapter 6. Surprisingly, however, decision-making through a societal cost–benefit analysis shows little explicit attention for the topic of reliability. Our theoretical framework for trustworthiness in societal cost–benefit analyses has been applied to the case of the Utrecht *Uithof line*. For the construction of this line, the Dutch Ministry of Infrastructure and Environment provided €110 million, with the condition that the societal cost–benefit analysis had to have a positive outcome. In other words, it should be a socially profitable project. The core of our approach is the focus on traveller effects, while reliability indicators often focus on supply, i.e., the vehicles. Through this approach, we show for the *Uithof line* project that the expected reliability amounts to about two-thirds of the total expected earnings. Without expressing these benefits, the societal cost–benefit analysis score would not have been positive for the light rail variant, as well as for other high-quality variants, such as 'bus rapid transit' (BRT).

Unfortunately, a smooth planning of light rail projects isn't self-evident, as we find out (not for the first time in this book) in Chapter 7. Urban development projects are always complex, especially when there is an infrastructural component. Unfortunately, many projects for tramways follow a slow and complicated course. Even if a new tram is successful, in many cases the underlying planning process has been extremely difficult.

The question is how to deal with failure and risk factors. Our cases involve lessons for an improved approach to light rail and other projects for high-quality public transport. A general lesson is to focus primarily on the 'why' of the project, instead of on the 'how' and the 'what'. Traditionally, most of the work is done on the latter, in any case in the majority of the 61 cases discussed in this book. As a result, the underlying argumentation is insufficient. The lesson, therefore, is that the 'why' of a project needs to be constantly elaborated, exposed and communicated.

In addition, project management of light rail projects should have a flexible, incremental form of planning. However, in the majority of the cases examined in this book, the project management chooses a rational planning. The projects with a complicated, integrated contract form are the worst. In particular, the DBFMO projects (Design, Build, Finance, Maintain, Operate) are characterized by a technocratic belief in rational planning. Most of these projects suffer greatly from the hectic, unreliable practice. Not always, but often, things go wrong. The Dutch case of *RegioTram* Groningen is an example.

It is wise to minimize the size of a project and to work as much as possible with proven technologies. It is also good practice to realize that is difficult to stop a project when a part of it is already in use. This approach is obviously difficult when using complex long-term contracts. In this regard, the differences between the *RegioTram* Groningen and the *Uithof line* projects are evident. The first project was characterized by an 'all or nothing' approach. The second project was a success, thanks to a series of preliminary and partial projects.

It is therefore wise to keep the first stage of a project as small as possible. However, the spatial and social environments of many projects require an approach that is as comprehensive as possible in the later stages. This implies a socially committed project management, an opportunistic stakeholder management and, especially, an unconventional approach to politics and governance. When these conditions are not met, things can go wrong, as became painfully clear in Groningen.

We present our conclusions in Chapter 8 with the concept of Smart City. In our view, cities are only successful if their infrastructures, networks and facilities are truly embedded in society. Also, a light rail system is successful only when it is really used. This social embedding is a condition for the successful completion of a project.

Unfortunately, of the 61 cases in this book, many light rail projects have become stranded in recent years. The relatively high number of failures in England is striking, while other European countries have also had to take their losses. There are many reasons for this, but our conclusion is that ultimately a lack of social foundation, combined with a too technocratic approach, should be identified as the main cause of failure. A Smart City is not so much a city where technology is offered to its inhabitants, but a city in which technology has social support and is then valued and used. Only then will investments in the city be sustainable.

New Tram of Athens Transforms City

Landscape architect Martin Knuijt has made a plan for the redevelopment of the centre of the Greek capital with his office OKRA (Utrecht, The Netherlands). The *Rethink Athens* project offers a solution to some of the current urban problems in Athens. Knuijt mentions too many vacancies, too much traffic, too little urban green and too little coherent public space. His plan provides for the adaptation and redevelopment of public space in the centre of Athens. For example, the busy Panepistimiou boulevard is transformed with a tramway, green strips, pavements, supply space and a two-way bicycle path. These zones are not sharply separated from each other. Sometimes there is a small difference in height, but mostly there are only differences in materials, colour and shape.

Impression of the renovated Syntagma Square in the heart of Athens. *(Image by OKRA.)*

The main question from opponents of the plan in the Greek capital is: 'If traffic is no longer crossing the six lanes of the Panepistimiou boulevard, where is it going?' 'A good question', says Martin Knuijt in an interview with some of the authors of this book. 'I think it isn't much of a problem, though. More than half of the car traffic doesn't have a destination downtown. Two parallel streets

New Tram of Athens Transforms City—cont'd

will undoubtedly get more traffic, but the new tramway will also transport some of the travellers. Just as a new road attracts new traffic, the closing of a road will reduce the car traffic throughout the area; simply because the journey will take too long. In this way, much traffic will disappear. Our experience in other cities is: just let the problem solve itself.'

The new tramway enhances the public realm and will carry former car drivers. *(Image by OKRA.)*

Our 61 Cases

In this book, 61 cases of light rail projects worldwide are scrutinized. Our overview offers a brief description of all cases labelled with the case-project's most important city. When a case-project has been failed or mothballed, the year of ending has been added with the following dagger symbol (†).

- **Aachen/Aix-la-Chapelle, Germany (2013 †), *CampusBahn*.** Tram project in Germany, like our other German case Hamburg, shown as an example of laborious planning. Both projects failed twice.
- **Almaty, Kazakhstan, *LRT*.** Our new example of integrated contract formation. Also one of our TOD cases. Based on recent fieldwork.
- **Antwerp-Deurne, Belgium, *Pegasus/Brabo I*.** Project in Flanders for extension of the existing tramway network. One of our case studies into integrated contract formation.

Continued

Our 61 Cases—cont'd

- **Athens, Greece, 'Re-think Athens'.** Urban renewal design scheme, including extension of existing tramway into the city centre. An excellent example of integration of urban planning and urban mobility.
- **Barcelona, Spain *Trambaix/Trambesòs*.** This new tramway entails two separate networks. Both are analysed as examples of TOD.
- **Bristol, UK (2004 †), *Supertram*.** Plan for a new light rail system in the urban region of Bristol. Staged as a case of a laborious planning process.
- **Casablanca, Morocco, *Tramway*.** Our first case in Northern Africa. Shows state-of-the-art technology and knowledge from France. An excellent example of French-style TOD.
- **Detroit, Michigan, US, *M-1 Rail Line*.** Project for a new tramway in downtown Detroit. This is an American case that illustrates the possible social aims and effects of light rail.
- **Dubai, UAE.** Our showcase in the Middle East. Dubai set a standard for light rail and TOD. Inspired neighbours like Abu Dhabi (UAE), Doha (Qatar) and Lusail (Qatar).
- **Dublin, Ireland, *Luas*.** Plan for a new light rail system called 'Luas' (Irish for 'Speed') in the urban region of Dublin. Staged as a case of laborious planning. However, eventually, after much political troubles the Irish capital gets its necessary tramway network.
- **Edinburgh, UK, *Trams*.** Our showcase from Scotland on faltering planning and disputes on contracts. Eventually the first, however curtailed stage became a reality.
- **Edmonton, Alberta, Canada, *LRT*.** Pioneer light rail project in Canada. The first light rail project of its kind in America (April 1978). Features TOD.
- **Groningen, Netherlands (2012 †), *RegioTram*.** This project is one of our three main cases. It's a source for many of our lessons on how to avoid technocratic approaches.
- **Hasselt-Maastricht, Belgium, *Spartacus*, Stage 1.** Project for a regional tramway. The Flanders section of this project poses as a case of special contract formation.
- **Hamburg, Germany (2012 †).** Tram project in Germany, like our other German case Aachen (Aix-la-Chapelle) shown as an example of laborious planning. As said earlier, both projects failed twice.
- **Jaén, Spain (2011 †), *El Tranvía*.** A Spanish urban tramway project, closed after a short period of operation. Mothballed ever since. Certainly an example of laborious planning.
- **Jerusalem, Israel, *CityPass*.** Controversial tramway project. Our own field-work in Jerusalem revealed this project as an obvious example of laborious planning.

Our 61 Cases—cont'd

- **Kaohsiung, Taiwan, *Circular Line*.** Our Asian state-of-the-art light rail and TOD case. The first light rail system in Taiwan with at least two more to come (New Taipei City and Taichung). The case underlined the importance of our Asian fieldworks.
- **Kiel, Germany (2013 †), *StadtRegionalBahn*.** A very special tram-train case in the urban region of this German harbour city, that closed its former tram system when the new tram of Nantes (France, 1985) started running. Like many tram-train schemes this project failed too.
- **La Réunion, France DROM (2010 †), *tram-train*.** Project for a big regional tramway in an overseas territory of France. Extremely difficult planning was the subject of our investigation on site. Our conclusion: overambitiousness killed this scheme.
- **Leeds, UK (2004 †), *Supertram*.** Plan for a new light rail system in the city of Leeds. Staged as a case of a long and laborious planning process.
- **Leiden, Netherlands (2012 †), *RijnGouwelijn*.** This Dutch showcase light rail project is compared with projects that applied integrated contracts. Second, the *RijnGouwelijn* is staged as a victim of laborious planning and incoherent political decision making that eventually killed the project. The third part of this case is the tram-train pilot operation of light rail within a heavy rail environment on a section of the envisaged system (2003–09).
- **Léon, Spain (2012 †), *Tren-tran*.** Project for a regional tram-train system. Halfway through construction the project was shut down due to sudden and unexpected financial cuts. From then on it has been mothballed and there is still no view on restarting (situation 2016).
- **Liverpool, UK (2005–08 †), *Merseytram*.** Plan for a new light rail system in the city. In the end not built, like many other UK projects, due to laborious planning and politics.
- **London, Croydon, UK, *Tramlink*.** This successful tramway project in the London metropolis serves as one of our peculiar contract formation cases.
- **London, UK (2008 †) *Cross River Tram*.** Plan for a new tramway through the core of central London. Again, the usual UK style of laborious planning and politics hit the project, though cancelled in 2008 due to funding problems.
- **London, Uxbridge, UK (2008 †), *West London Tram (West London Transit)*.** Plan for a tramway in the western part of London metropolis. Didn't get a fair chance. Laborious planning and politics of London boroughs prevented continuation of the project.

Continued

Our 61 Cases—cont'd

LA's light rail in Pasadena envisages TOD at Del Mar station (2007).

- **Los Angeles, California, US, *Pacific Electric/Metro*.** Our double-case in California: the historic and contemporary light rail systems of Greater Los Angeles with their many overlaps. This is one of our most important TOD cases from the US. It is also a case that exhibits social effects of light rail.
- **Lyon, France, *Tramway*.** New urban tramway system complementary to the existing metro system. This case is used to illustrate the value of a new tramway despite the existence of a metro system.
- **Lyon, France, *Rhônexpress*.** Project for a dedicated airport tramway and a case of integrated contract formation.
- **Lyon, France, *Tram-train de l'ouest lyonnais*.** Light rail scheme for improving the service on the regional railway from Lyon Saint-Paul station to Sain-Bel. This is one of our cases of light rail operation within a heavy rail environment.
- **Liège, Belgium, *Le Tram*.** Project for new urban tramway, that aimed at integrated contract formation. Delayed due to violation of financial requirements of Eurostat, but still ongoing (situation in 2016).
- **Luxembourg (2004 †).** Failed project for a tram-train system in the urban region of Luxembourg's capital. Indeed a case of laborious planning. Subsequently followed by a project for an urban tramway in the city (under construction, situation in 2016).

Our 61 Cases—cont'd

- **Manchester, UK, *Metrolink*.** The biggest light rail system in England. Strong case of successful commercial property development in combination with a new tramway. Also mirrors our Utrecht cases.
- **Nice, France, *Ligne 1*.** Excellent urban tramway project based on classic contracts, hence, used as a reference for our study on integrated contract formation.
- **Nottingham, UK, *Nottingham Express Transit, Line 1/Lines 2 & 3*.** Impressive urban tramway project based on complicated, though successful, contract formation. This case also entails the follow-up project for two new tramways.
- **Olsztyn, Poland, *Tramwaje*.** Our 'mirror-case' for Groningen *RegioTram*. Eventually the tramway project of Olsztyn was successful due to a pragmatic and flexible approach.
- **Oranjestad, Aruba, *Arutram*.** An urban renewal project, including a new tramway connection between the cruise terminal and city centre.
- **Paris, France, *T1*.** The first new tramway in Paris metropolis. Our example of a pioneer project, that eventually was built and proved to be successful after many years of laborious planning.
- **Paris, France, *T4*.** A conversion from heavy rail to light rail case in the metropolitan area of Paris. This is the first fully French tram-train project.
- **Portland, Oregon, US, *Metro/Streetcar*.** Urban regional light rail system, completed with an urban tramway (streetcar). This is our most important case in the US on TOD.
- **Portsmouth, UK (2004–06 †), *South Hampshire Rapid Transit*.** Failed project for a new light rail system in the urban region of Portsmouth on the English coast. A tragic case of years of laborious planning.
- **Queensland, Australia, *Gold Coast Light Rail*.** One of the two of our successful TOD cases in Australia. A cutting-edge project.
- **Reims, France, *Le Tramway*.** The first urban tramway project in France using a fully integrated contract (DBFMO), hence, an excellent case of special contract formation.
- **Rio de Janeiro, Brazil, *VLT Carioca*.** Our first case in South America. This new system uses state-of-the-art French technology and features 'Olympic' TOD.
- **Saarbrücken, Germany, *Saarbahn*.** A new light rail system in the urban region of Saarbrücken, the capital of the state of Saarland. Could have been our German tram-train case, however, it is staged here as a case of delay and laborious planning.
- **Stavanger, Norway (2012 †), *Bybanen*.** Failed project in Norway for a new tram-train system in the urban region of Stavanger-Sandnes. Our fieldwork-based case of a prolonged and laborious planning process.

Continued

Our 61 Cases—cont'd

- **Stockholm, Sweden, *Spårväg City***. Example of an urban tramway project in Sweden, initially failed due to improvident use of an integrated contract, eventually successful after reframing the project into a classic assignment.
- **Strasbourg, France, *Ligne A***. An iconic French urban tramway project. Staged here as an excellent case proving the economic impact of light rail on city centres.
- **Sydney, Australia, *CBD and South East Light Rail* & *Inner West Light Rail***. One of the two of our successful TOD cases in Australia. Sydney sets a standard for light rail in Australia.
- **The Hague/Rotterdam, Netherlands, *RandstadRail***. The biggest light rail project of the Netherlands and one of our three main cases.
- **The Hague Region, Netherlands, *Line 19***. A Dutch tramway project in the urban region of The Hague (Haaglanden). This case of classic contracting is compared with projects using integrated contracts.
- **Toyama, Japan, *Portram***. The Japanese showcase light rail project and one of our TOD cases in Asia, intensively explored during fieldwork.
- **Tel Aviv, Israel, *Red Line***. Ambitious light rail project in Israel with metro characteristics. Our case entails the failed first tender on the basis of an integrated contract. Meanwhile the project has been restarted.

Utrecht, Netherlands, *SUNIJ*, the LRVs of the first generation, high floor, though in renewed livery (2013).

Our 61 Cases—cont'd

- **Utrecht, Netherlands, *SUNIJ*.** Our Dutch 'reference case' light rail project. This pioneer features TOD and connections to new towns in the Utrecht region.
- **Utrecht, Netherlands (1995 †).** Terminated project for an inner city tramway. A distinctive example of laborious planning in a Dutch city.
- **Utrecht, Netherlands, *Uithof line*.** The third case from Utrecht and one of our three main cases from Holland with comprehensive proof of the additional value of light rail.
- **Valenciennes, France, *Le Tramway*.** New tram system in the city of Valenciennes and its region. Our case in the north of France that inspired the *RegioTram* project in Groningen (Netherlands).
- **Vélez-Málaga, Spain (2012 †), *Tranvía*.** One of the various new urban tramways in Spain. However, closed after less than 6 years of operation. Deserves a place in our series of laborious planning processes. Still mothballed (situation in 2016).
- **Zhuhai, China, *Urban Rail Transit*.** Our first (ongoing) case in China. This new system uses cutting-edge light rail technology though features weak TOD characteristics.
- **Zwolle-Kampen, Netherlands (2013 †).** Our prize-winning conversion-to-tramway study. Implementation has been seriously considered, though finally replaced by an improved heavy rail project.

CHAPTER 2

What is Light Rail?

This book is about high quality public transport as a public resource worth investing in. Light rail is an excellent example of this kind of public transport, usually associated with urban rail-based transport such as tramways, metros or light trains. However, for a better understanding of the operation and value of light rail for a city, an accurate definition is required. Light rail is often a so-called 'container concept' that refers to all kinds of public rail transport in the city, and also in urban and metropolitan regions. Beyond such a container concept, light rail in this book is reverted to the domain of 'neighboring' modalities such as the classic tram, new-generation trams, light metros and various forms of light regional trains.

2.1 DEFINITIONS

The term light rail dates from the mid-1970s. The Transportation Research Board (1978) offers the following definition: 'Light rail transit is a metropolitan electric railway system characterized by its ability to operate single cars or short trains along exclusive rights-of-way at ground level, on aerial structures, in subways or, occasionally, in streets, and to board and discharge passengers at track or car-floor level'.

With all due respect for the past, this definition does not satisfy us completely, especially because the urban planning and traffic-related implications of light rail differ from those of other modalities. In this definition, this is not adequately expressed. Take the example of a part of a city that is operated by light rail, for example, a shopping mall with adjacent facilities plus housing. In this case, the tramway is usually on ground level, there are grade intersections and the light rail vehicle (LRV) in some sections shares space with the remaining traffic, sometimes even with pedestrians. In this situation, there are about two or three stops, fully integrated in public space, and thus connected to the area via relatively short walking routes on the ground level, with no height differences.

In exactly the same situation, but then served by a metro or regional train, only one station would be available, most likely underground or

Light Rail Transit Systems
ISBN 978-0-12-814784-9
https://doi.org/10.1016/B978-0-12-814784-9.00002-5

elevated as an embankment or viaduct. Integration with the environment is not necessarily worse, but certainly different. In any event, public transport is less visible. But more important, the walking distances are greater and more difficult, because to get to or from the station, height differences must be overcome.

The tramway of Lyon uses 'classic' stops in de street.

In the case described in this book of the new urban tramway network for the city of Lyon (France), that is complementary to the existing metro system, these characteristics are obvious when one compares the urban situation and logistics of metro stations and tram stops, respectively.

The concept of light rail is usually located in a triangle, between train, tram and metro. But the differences are often unclear. Therefore, there are many misunderstandings about the meaning of the term 'light rail'; there is an undeniable confusion of tongues. This complicates thinking about the nature and necessity of light rail, and is an obstacle for consistent thinking and regulation.

Also, the concept is used in different ways. Often there is a focus on light vehicles or infrastructure, or a tram or metro-like operation. In general, light rail stands for a generally unspecified form of rail-bound public transport, somewhere in-between tram and metro, and possibly even in-between train and metro. This hybrid characteristic reflects the multiple use of light rail. Urban areas have increased in size, with the result that living, working and other activities are more widely spread. In this new context, light rail provides flexible, high-quality public transport, with less transfer and efficient adapted infrastructure.

In short, light rail is a container concept that includes trams and other types of rail-bound public transport. Moreover, the 'light' qualification does not relate to the weight of the used vehicles, but to the characteristics of infrastructure and operation. Thus, 'light' implies that infrastructure and associated operations can be flexibly integrated into urban environments.

Nevertheless, it is possible to accurately and precisely describe the relevant components and focus on a group of light rail applications, especially regiotram, express tram, and conventional tram, and in any case tram-train and metro-tram. We therefore propose the following definition:

Light rail is a rail-bound form of public transport that is used on the scale of the urban region and the city. In contrast to train and metro, light rail is suitable for integration to a certain extent in public space and, if desired, for mixing with regular road traffic.

In principle, train, tram and metro represent functionally and technically completely separate public transport infrastructures. The question now is how to more precisely characterize light rail, and especially to define the possible overlaps between the three neighboring modalities. To this end, we will use a strict distinction between infrastructure and vehicles on the one hand, and operation and use on the other hand. Subsequently we will focus on the performance and perception of light rail. For example, transport value and public appreciation are the result of the way infrastructure and light rail vehicles are operated and used. With the next three paragraphs we anticipate on the following chapters in this book.

Light Rail in a Glance

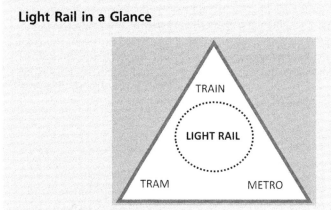

Figure 2.1 Light rail is situated in the domain of train, tram and metro.

Continued

Light Rail in a Glance—cont'd

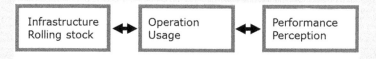

LIGHT RAIL

Figure 2.2 A triple distinction is essential for the characterization of light rail.

In principle, train, tram and metro represent functionally and technically separate types of public transport infrastructure. Light rail doesn't need dedicated infrastructure, but can use the three types of infrastructure available for urban rail-related public transport. However, tram infrastructure is most suitable for light rail operation (Figs 2.1 and 2.2).

- Light rail features some basic characteristics. Compared to train and metro rolling stock an LRV is generally smaller and lighter. The most characteristic feature of an LRV is the ability to mix in functional and legal terms with other traffic. This has a major influence on vehicle characteristics.

- Light rail operation typically allows (if desired) running across different types of infrastructure within a tram system, or from that system to the train or metro infrastructure. The range of such rail-based public transport services can extend to local, regional or even upper-regional levels. The focus of light rail operation, however, is the urban region.

- Light rail operation serves primarily for transport of persons. At intermodal nodes light rail stations and stops are linked to other modes of transport, like cars and bicycles, and other public transport, like buses. By using fixed infrastructure light rail structures the urban region served, hence, structures the urban region spatially, economically, environmentally and socially.

- Light rail performs well when its perception by the public is coherent and efficient. Naming and branding affect the experience and appreciation of a light rail system.

- Light rail is a rail-bound mode of public transport that is used on the scale of the urban region and the city. Contrary to rail and metro, light rail is by definition suitable for integration to a certain extent in public space and, if desired, to mix with regular road traffic.

2.2 INFRASTRUCTURE AND VEHICLES

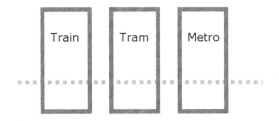

LIGHT RAIL

Figure 2.3 Three types of infrastructure: train: separated — tram: integrated — metro: closed.

Light rail as such has no dedicated infrastructure (Fig. 2.3), but it can use the three types of rail-based infrastructure available within urban contexts for tram, train and metro (see all details in Table 2.1).

Tramway infrastructure entails various forms. When necessary, tramways can be integrated within the public realm in general and other traffic lanes in particular. Grade crossings can have the status of a regular traffic intersection. According to our definition, it is obvious that tram infrastructure is by far the most appropriate for light rail operations.

In principle, railways for train operation represent fully separated infrastructure, normally with absolute priority at intersections with

Table 2.1 Infrastructure: Outline of Some Characteristics

	Light Rail	Regiotram	City Tram	Train	Metro
Surrounding	Integrated	Integrated	Integrated	Separated	Closed
Intersections	Few	Sometimes	Frequently	Less	Never
Priority	Frequently	C	Sometimes	Always	—
Distance between stops	0.4—2 km	0.4—1 km	0.2—0.6 km	5—100 km	0.4—0.8 km
Platforms	Low/high	Low/high	Low	Middle high	High
Security	Frequently	Frequently	Sometimes	Always	Always

other traffic. Metro infrastructure in principle is fully closed to other traffic, hence, normally there are no grade intersections with other traffic. Tunnels are usually associated with metro infrastructure. However, in this regard the absence of grade intersections is the ultimate feature and therefore the cheaper elevated sections are a common form of metro.

Sometimes the infrastructures of tram, metro or train look similar or almost identical, for example a tunnel, or a viaduct. However, decisively for system characteristics are not this kind of individual components, but overall system properties. This implies for trams that they are integrated in the urban realm. For train separated from public realm and for metro fully segregated from urban realm and other traffic.

Light rail vehicles have specific characteristics (see all details in Table 2.2). LRVs' ability to mix functionally and legally with other traffic is crucial to its vehicle characteristics. LRVs within Europe have an impact strength of 1500 kN or less, while 600 kN is common. Therefore, the distinction between light rail vehicles and heavy rail vehicles is distinct. In North America, the limit for impact strength is higher (3560 kN). Trains such as Stadler DMUs (1500 kN) are thus considered to be light rail vehicles.

Table 2.2 Vehicles: Outline of Some Characteristics

	Light Rail	Regiotram	Tram	Train	Metro
Length	30–120 m	30–75 m	25–75 m	80–350 m	25–80 m
Width	265 cm	240/265 cm	220/265 cm	265/300 cm	220/300 cm
Impact strength	≤1500 kN	≤1500 kN	≤600 kN	≥1500 kN	≤1500 kN
Average speed	45 km/h	30 km/h	15 km/h	≥60 km/h	30 km/h
Maximum speed	≤100 km/h	≤100 km/h	≤70 km/h	≥80 km/h	≤80 km/h
Floor height	Low/high	Low/high	Low	High	High
Number of doors	Average	Average	Average/more than average	Average/less than average	Many
Number of seats/standees	1/2	1/2	2/3	1/2 −4/none	3/4

LRVs in Europe are not wider than 2.65 m, almost without exception. North America also accepts wider vehicles. The optimal width and length of LRVs are related to integration requirements, in other words, the ways in which LRVs fit into the traffic environment. This also applies to many additional vehicle features, such as braking and boarding facilities.

Typically, differences between LRVs and various models of tram vehicles are minor, hence, there is no real distinction nor is there an obvious definition in this regard. This comes as no surprise since LRVs predominantly use tramway infrastructure. If the operation requires that LRVs also use train infrastructure, they will normally have to meet requirements and features that apply to heavy rail trains. The same happens when LRVs run on metro tracks.

Moreover, security and other relevant requirements can be met by adaptations to the ways in which LRVs are operated and used. In that case, vehicle adjustments may be limited or almost none. However, this kind of solution presupposes requirements being framed as performance requirements.

For the sake of completeness, heavy rail trains or metro vehicles require certain characteristics of trams or LRVs when allowed on the tramway infrastructure.

Examples of Urban Light Rail Infrastructures

Examples of six basic types of light rail infrastructure are determined. Each represents light rail infrastructure with particular characteristics regarding the way this infrastructure has been tailored to its urban environment.
- Traditional street-based;
- Shared-space;
- Traffic lane;
- Separate tramway;
- Metro style tramway;
- Railway for tram-train.

For each type a series of six elements are characterized: line (infrastructure), intersections (crossings), stops (in context), stations (if applied), facilities (e.g., shelter, parking), and alignment (relative to street pattern).

In practice, light rail infrastructure of a particular light rail line could be a combination of various types. Some of our cases, like the light rail system of *RandstadRail* in the Netherlands, combine several line types in the infrastructure. Most new-generation tramways combine the use of shared-space, traffic lanes

Continued

Examples of Urban Light Rail Infrastructures—cont'd

and separated infrastructure (e.g., our cases in Dublin, Lyon (*Tramway*), Strasbourg, and Valenciennes).

Traditional Street-Based

Line: fully integrated with regular traffic;
Intersections: no special features other than for regular traffic;
Stops: on pavements, sometimes platform within a pavement zone;
Stations: not feasible;
Facilities: sometimes without shelters or any other facilities;
Alignment: according to street pattern.

Old, street-based tramway in Almaty (Kazakhstan). Relates to our case about the light rail project that aims to upgrade parts of this old infrastructure.

Shared-Space

Line: specifically integrated with a limited number of other traffic forms (e.g., pedestrians);
Intersections: could be part of the shared-space zone;
Stops: integrated in the shared-space, sometimes platform distinguished (physically or visually only);

Examples of Urban Light Rail Infrastructures—cont'd

Stations: not feasible;
Facilities: modest, sometimes comprehensive (e.g., cycle parking facilities);
Alignment: according to the street pattern.

Second-generation French urban tramway within the public realm of the city of Reims. In this historic context, instead of conventional overhead wire, 'Alimentation par le Sol' (APS) is applied. Moreover, Reims represents one of our cases on integrated contracts.

Traffic Lane

Line: separated from other traffic's lane(s), e.g., by painted line or curb;
Intersections: at the same grade as all other traffic, possibly equipped with traffic lights;
Stops: separated most likely (side platforms parallel to sidewalks);
Stations: not very common;
Facilities: modest, sometimes comprehensive (e.g., cycle parking facilities);
Alignment: according to the (main) street pattern.

Continued

Examples of Urban Light Rail Infrastructures—cont'd

A separated tram lane in the city Edinburgh (UK), which is shared with many buses. Moreover, Edinburgh represents one of our cases on faltering planning and disputes on contracts.

Separate Tramway

Line: fully separated from other traffic, own track bed;

Intersections: at grade, commonly equipped with traffic lights (possibly with barriers), sometimes by viaduct or tunnel;

Stops: separated, side platforms parallel to sidewalks, or island platforms within the two tracks;

Stations: possible, e.g., construction around island platforms;

Facilities: comprehensive, shelters and possibly more (e.g., Park & Ride, cycle parking);

Alignment: according to the main street pattern, or fully independent.

Tramway on own track bed along a wide street in the city of Berlin (Germany).

Examples of Urban Light Rail Infrastructures—cont'd

Metro Style Tramway

Line: fully separated from other traffic, independent infrastructure;
Intersections: by viaduct or tunnels (smaller crossings possible at grade with barriers);
Stops: possible, though platforms separated from adjacent space;
Stations: most likely, underground or elevated structure (with entrances);
Facilities: comprehensive (station hall, ticket machines, amenities, etc.);
Alignment: mainly independent.

Metro-style light rail at one of the Rotterdam-based stations of our case *RandstadRail*.

Railway for Tram-Train

Line: along autonomous heavy railway (of all forms);
Intersections: according with the crossings of autonomous heavy railway (of all forms);
Stops: possible, though platforms separated from adjacent space;
Stations: according with the stations of heavy railway (of all forms);
Facilities: comprehensive, according with the heavy rail stations (of all forms);
Alignment: fully independent.

Continued

Examples of Urban Light Rail Infrastructures—cont'd

Light rail vehicle (LRV) on a heavy railway at Gouda (Netherlands), during a pilot from our case *RijnGouwelijn*.

Examples of Light Rail Vehicles

Four basic types of LRV have been determined. Each represents distinguished characteristics of today's LRVs regarding the way these vehicles are tailored to their use in urban environments.

- Conventional urban tram vehicle;
- New-generation low-floor urban tram vehicle;
- High-floor light rail vehicle;
- Tram-train vehicle.

The sizes (common widths—lengths) and capacity of each example/type of vehicle are provided. Some features are noted that highlight each of these four types, and some notes on common examples are included.

In practice the variety of light rail vehicles is much larger and more complex than is suggested here by means of this limited example typology. Some of our cases, like the light rail systems of London/Croydon (UK), Lyon *Rhônexpress* (France) and *RandstadRail* (Netherlands) are operated by trams that feature overlapping characteristics.

Functional length and capacity increase when vehicles are coupled in two or three sets. The maximum length of a 'train' is commonly 75 m (when restricted due to street-operation sections).

Examples of Light Rail Vehicles—cont'd

Conventional Urban Tram Vehicle
Dimensions: 2.20/2.40/2.50 m. Min. 15 m.

Capacity: min. c.100 passengers.

Features: many forms, frequently revamped, redesigned, or used as secondhand low-budget cars.

Examples: used in a couple of hundred cities worldwide, notably in Europe.

PCC-car series 1100 built by La Brugeoise et Nivelles (now Bombardier) according to the design of the famous American 'Presidents' Conference Committee' model (1929). These trams dominated the tramways in The Hague, Netherlands during the first post-war years (and other European cities like Antwerp and Ghent in Belgium). In addition, North America East-Europa was massively served by this kind of tram, built by the well-known Tatra factory in Prague (in former Czechoslovakia). Many of them got a second life as maintaining vehicles or tourist trams (see photo). *(Image by Kees Pronk.)*

New-Generation Low-Floor Urban Tram Vehicle
Dimensions: 2.40/2.65 m. Min. 30 m.

Capacity: 250–300 passengers.

Continued

Examples of Light Rail Vehicles—cont'd

Features: one or more articulations, 60%—100% low floor, and dozens of technical variations and forms.

Examples: in all European second-generation tramways in Europe; also examples in new recent American systems.

The Urbos 3 manufactured by the Spanish firm CAF for Kaohsiung (Taiwan) is a cutting-edge 100% low-floor tram, delivered here as a five-section vehicle with three bogies, two of which are powered. These trams for Kaohsiung are bidirectional, air-conditioned, 34 m long and 2.65 m wide with a capacity of 250 passengers, including 64 seated. A special feature is the CAF-developed 'Acumulador de Carga Rapida' (ACR) system that allows the vehicle to run without overhead wires.

High-Floor Light Rail Vehicle

Dimensions: 2.65 m. Min. 28 m.

Capacity: min. 183 passengers.

Features: Germany's invention of 'Stadtbahn B' (Duewag, Siemens) and 'U2' (Duewag, Wegmann, Siemens). High floor, one or two articulations, numerous variations and forms produced, including state-of-the-art low-floor models (e.g., LRV Siemens S70 in Houston, Texas, US).

Examples: Classic Germans are Stadtbahn B in Cologne and U2 in Frankfurt. The U2 is also the founding father of North America's first generation of new

Examples of Light Rail Vehicles—cont'd

light rail systems like our case in Edmonton (Alberta, Canada), but also San Diego (California, US) and various others.

Utrecht (Netherlands) is home to a first generation of high-floor vehicles designed according to the Stadtbahn B model. From 2020, all of these cars will be replaced by low-floor Urbos 3 CAF LRVs.

Tram-Train Vehicle

Dimensions: 2.65 m. Min. 28 m.

Capacity: min. c.200 passengers.

Features: Always has full heavy rail compatibility (i.e., technically and legally), many variations and types.

Examples: The regional tram-train system of Karslruhe is the founding father of this kind of vehicles. The first series here (1992) is based on the Stadtbahn B model. Later series feature low-floor sections. Tram-train vehicles that substantially share tracks with heavy rail trains are an exclusive European phenomenon. For instance in the urban regions of other German cities (Saarbrücken, Chemnitz), and in France (Mulhouse). Recent examples are Cádiz, Spain (2017) and Rotherham, UK (2018).

Continued

Examples of Light Rail Vehicles—cont'd

The Citadis Dualis manufactured by Alstom has become the standard tram-train vehicle in France. In the region of Lyon this type of LRV is used on the Saint-Paul–Sain-Bel railway (see also our case). Other supplied regions in France are Nantes and Île de France (Paris). Various new systems are planned. The Citadis Dualis is available with various technical options: width (2.40/2.66 m), length (42/52 m), dual voltage (25 kV/750 V, 1500 V/750 V). Shock resistance is always in compliance with EN 15227C-III standards. Maximum speed 100 km/h.

2.3 OPERATION AND USE

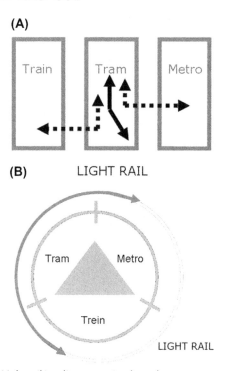

Figure 2.4 (A and B) Light rail implies operation based on one or more rail infrastructures.

Table 2.3 Operations: Outline of Hybrid Modes and Their Catchments

	Light Rail	Regiotram	Tram	Train	Metro
Catchment	Local/ regional	Local/ regional	Local	≥Regional	Local
Line length	10—80 km	10—40 km	5—20 km	≥20 km	5—30 km
Track sharing	Often	Mostly	Sometimes	Rarely	Rarely

Overview

	Light Rail	Regiotram	Tram	Train	Metro
	Tram Regiotram Tram-train Tram-metro Metro-tram Train-metro	Tram Tram-train Tram-metro Metro-tram	Tram-train	Train-tram	Metro-tram Tram-metro

Light rail operation allows through running on different types of infra-structure within a tramway system, or from that system to a train or metro infrastructure, if necessary (Fig. 2.4 A and B). The range of such public transport services can extend to local, regional or even upper-regional levels. The urban region, however, remains the focus of common light rail operation (see overview in Table 2.3).

The dominant form of light rail is fast and enhanced tramways, frequently branded as RegioTram. As mentioned earlier, the distinction between LRVs and trams is blurred. Classic trams, modern low-floor trams and larger regionally operated trams offer a wide variety of light rail that even includes hybrid modes called 'tram-train' and 'tram-metro'. In the first case, train infrastructure is linked to a tramway network. This link allows through running of LRVs on heavy railways. Often this kind of operation involves track sharing, that is, LRVs and heavy rail trains sharing the same railway. Moreover it is feasible for LRVs to use a heavy railway without heavy rail train operation being present. In such a case LRV's are still operated under the technical and legal conditions of heavy rail. Once it is decided to abolish these technical and legal con-straints, the traditional heavy railway is de facto converted into a tramway.

Tram-metro represents an operation in which LRVs share track with metro vehicles on a metro infrastructure. In contrast, metro-tram means through operation of metro vehicles on tramways. Similarly train-tram represents situations where trains run through on parts of a tramway.

The distinction between a tram-train and train-tram is considerable. It is less difficult to use a tram within the context of a separate train infrastructure than to allow a train within relatively tight tramways closely linked to an urban environment and the use of that environment. The distinction between tram-metro and train-metro is less compelling. This is because the characteristics of tram and metro vehicles do not always differ significantly. However, the operation of trams differs significantly from metro operation, especially in technical terms.

For the sake of completeness, two other modes of operation must be mentioned here: metro vehicles through running on heavy railways (metro-train) and the reverse, trains running through on metro railways (train-metro). Both forms of integration and track sharing are not strictly referred to as light rail. In the case of trains with LRV characteristics (e.g., trains from Swiss light railways), the situation reflects light rail.

Light rail operation serves primarily for transport of passengers. Users of this kind of public transport include different target groups, distinguished by category (forced, choice and potential traveler) and by type (commuting, residential, shopping, recreation, etc.). Historically light rail for freight transport was common practice. Despite ideas and discussions on the reintroduction of freight tramways in urban areas (e.g., Amsterdam, Netherlands and Paris, France) few projects were successful (e.g., Zurich, Switzerland and Dresden, Germany). The freight tram of Zurich, branded as 'Cargotram' started operation in 2003. The tram collects and transports household waste. Two years earlier the 'CarGoTram' in Dresden started operation transporting car parts from a station at the fringe of the city into the centre-based Volkswagen manufacturing plant. The service was terminated in March 2016, but resumed a year later when production of a new type of automobile was started.

Table 2.4 Urban Planning and Design: Outline of TOD

	Light Rail	Regiotram	Tram	Train	Metro
Reach	3—30 km	3—20 km	3—10 km	≥10 km	3—10 km
TOD Overview	++	++	++	+	+
Line	X	X	X		
Stop	X	X	X	X	
Station	X	X		X	X

The operation of light rail ultimately involves a contribution to mobility in a broader context. Its use is (or should be) geared to the use of other modes of public transport, as well as individual mobility, notably cars and bicycles. The use of light rail is inextricably linked to the function of the entire transport chain, for all modalities, and at all scale levels — however, with emphasis on transport linked to cities and their urban regions.

Light rail is geared to other methods of transport in so-called intermodal nodes or transit centres, which entail stations and stops where light rail and all other transport meet and are linked together, allowing smooth transfer from tram to bus or train, or from tram, bus and train to car, bicycle and other individual or public means of transport.

Beyond mere transport, fixed light rail infrastructure also serves urban planning (see Table 2.4). Light rail structures the city and its urban region, in an economic and social sense. Operation of high-quality public transport can be used to strengthen economic centres, and to prevent social segregation. Locally, light rail can be used to improve the quality and use of public space. Light rail in this way is a kind of urban design and planning, rather than just a means of public transport. In this regards so-called transit oriented development (TOD) is increasingly being used. Spatial development is thus linked to stations, stops, and their vicinities. Within urban centres development is often structured along a string of local light rail stops.

Moreover light rail's role in urban planning and design focuses on various environmental aspects. In this sense light rail operation becomes an expression of 'green politics'. In itself, the structural impact of light rail already implies an environmental benefit, expressed in the prevention of urban sprawl and increasing (car) mobility. Locally, light rail improves urban health. It reduces the amount of small particles, while at the same time the overall noise level is lowered and nuisance due to vibrations is reduced.

All those effects of light rail operation (in domains of transport, urban planning, environment, etc.) justify underlining the importance of public transport. For these reasons light rail is often used as a means for a city or an urban region to distinguish itself. Light rail then becomes a brand or logo.

Light Rail in Action

The operational characteristics of light rail are reflected in its many uses. Our series of action-examples illustrates and exemplifies the wide range of light rail situations and forms in this regard.

- Action 1 — Vintage light rail in a museum and tourist setting.

Historic light rail vehicle (HTM 58) ran once on the Dutch regional urban system between The Hague and Leiden (closed 1961), and now occasionally runs on the museum tramway of Arnhem (Netherlands).

- Action 2 — Three examples of the same type of Light Rail Vehicle (LRV) on three different infrastructures.

Light Rail in Action—cont'd

Coupled set of LRVs (metro-style LRVs from Rotterdam) sharing same infrastructure with tram-style LRVs of *RandstadRail* (The Hague, Netherlands).

Coupled set of LRVs on metro infrastructure (*RandstadRail*, Rotterdam, Netherlands).

Continued

Light Rail in Action—cont'd

Coupled set of LRVs on former railway infrastructure (*RandstadRail*, Rotterdam region, Netherlands).

- Action 3 — Another type of vehicle at work on a heavy railway, though still an LRV (Light Rail Vehicle) according to the American standards.

The regional system of Groningen, Netherlands (see also our case *RegioTram*), is operated with diesel-electric trains from type GTW ('Gelenktriebwagen' from Stadler) on railway infrastructure. Similar vehicles are operated tramway-style on street sections in Camden, New Jersey (US).

Light Rail in Action—cont'd

- Action 4 — Some trams get a second life as maintenance vehicles.

A PCC car (according to the the design of the famous American 'Presidents' Conference Committee' model) from The Hague (Netherlands) operates as a monitor tram for the *RandstadRail* light rail system on a former heavy rail section. *(Image by Kees Pronk.)*

- Action 5 — Twice light rail under construction.

Some road-based vehicles mounted on tracks for construction of tramway *T3* in Paris (situation July 2012).

Continued

Light Rail in Action—cont'd

Catenary construction work at the site of a large depot facility in The Hague (Netherlands). *(Image by Kees Pronk.)*

- Action 6 — Four examples of a light rail set within eye-catching sceneries.

LRV in the city of Bergen (Norway) matches beautifully with the surrounding scenery of this historic city and its mountains ('Bergen' means 'mountains') (situation in April 2017).

Light Rail in Action—cont'd

Tracks of the light rail system in Houston (Texas, US) intersect an excellent shaped fountain construction.

The new tramway of Bilbao obviously also represents an urban green project of high quality.

Continued

Light Rail in Action—cont'd

One of the regional tramways of Innsbruck (Austria) is captured in a yellow-flower-dominated scenery.

- Action 7 — Two stations in Asia at work.

In Zhangjiang on the eastern side of Shanghai city a 'tram sur tires' arrived at its terminus. This French, one-rail-only technology is developed by Translohr as 'tram sur pneu', actually a hybrid tram—bus mode. Besides, the real light rail project in Shanghai also entails French technology, e.g., LRVs constructed by Alstom, and is implemented for the new Songjiang tram network (2017). *(Image by Axel Kuehn.)*

Light Rail in Action—cont'd

Combino tram from Europe (Siemens) fits beautifully in this busy Japanese tram station in Hiroshima. An original local tram is also calling.

- Action 8 — Two examples of the same type of Light Rail Vehicle (LRV) on two different systems, however, with the same operator.

LRV (manufactured by Kinki Sharyo) is running on the elevated section at 8th street of the Hudson—Bergen light rail system operated by NJ Transit (Hoboken, New Jersey, US).

Continued

Light Rail in Action—cont'd

A similar LRV, but now running in the streets of Newark (New Jersey, US), also operated by NJ Transit.

- Action 9 — Two examples of a light rail former-Soviet-Union-style underlines the rich though ambiguous history of light rail in all parts of the world.

The express tramway in Volgograd (Russia) opened in different stages between 1972 and 1976. Two twin-sets of Tatra type T-3 cars are running near the southern entrance to the tunnel section.

Light Rail in Action—cont'd

An oil-refinery factory in the town of Krasnoarmeysk (Russia), built a new tramway opened in 1958. A tram in the background is passing a local market.

2.4 PERFORMANCE AND PERCEPTION

Due to typical light rail features (urban, high transport quality, high comfort, visually pleasing, etc.) this form of public transport is more attractive than most. For instance, light rail's transport value is higher than generally expected, assessed or even calculated. This phenomenon is referred to as the 'rail bonus' — which can often be around 15%. For various reasons, light rail performs better than other forms of public transport. It is more reliable, faster and more comfortable, and it has a greater capacity than buses, which generally do not allow longer units than 18 m (only in special cases are double-articulated 24-m buses practically usable).

According to our rule of thumb light rail (and high quality bus) allows travelling intervals of up to 5 min. Under specific conditions this can be reduced for light rail. For example: our case of the *Uithof line* (see Chapter 6)

Table 2.5 Transport Demand: Outline Minimum West European Values (Number of Passengers)

	Light Rail	Regiotram	Tram	Train	Metro
Overview					
Average	Various	20,000/day	15,000/day	Various	50,000/day
Rush city	1000 p/h	1000 p/h	1000 p/h	...	≫ 1000 p/h
Rush region	600 p/h	600 p/h	600 p/h	...	...

in theory allows 4 min. Since most Uithof-bound travellers are boarding at the first station of the line. Our case of *RandstadRail* allows 2.5 min on the common section of RR3 and RR4. This performance is possible due to the available former heavy rail infrastructure as well as a series of operational measures (see Chapter 5). However, generally calculated capacity and related performance regarding transport demand (Table 2.5) should be based on a travelling interval of 5 min and additionally on 2/3 of the theoretical vehicle capacity. Please note that when multiple lines are combined on a trunk line (e.g., in city centre) the introduction of light rail can be considered with lower numbers on each of the individual lines. Another note: one should not confuse transport volume on the busiest route with volume of the whole line; the latter volume is, of course, larger. A final note: the above numbers relate to considerations for justifying light rail are linked to West European practices. Numbers elsewhere can be lower (e.g., in US) or higher (e.g., in China).

In addition to transport performance, light rail affects cities and urban regions in various other ways. Impacts on the value of land and real estate have been found to be plausible in various studies. It is also likely that the quality of urban retail is enhanced by light rail. For instance, French new tramway cities showed a 'gentrification' of retail in their inner cities shortly after the introduction of new tramways. Finally, light rail could affect the social fabric of cities. Many light rail projects (notably in Western Europe and the US) aim to enhance social inclusion. Though the social importance of sound public transport is quite evident, it's not sure yet whether its performance really entails social change.

Yet another effect of light rail relates to issues of safety and security. Contrary to what is often assumed, safety and security are not properties of light rail amenities, infrastructures and the vehicles themselves. On the other hand, they are the result of interactions between light rail facilities (including services) and the ways of usage by citizens. In other words, safety and security are first of all performances linked to usage of light rail, and behavior of passengers, non-passengers, and even criminals or vandals, and in the case of traffic safety behavior of car drivers and other traffic participants, notably pedestrians.

Finally, some remarks on the branding and legibility of light rail systems. The perception of these systems is highly dependent on branding. Typically, logos are used, whose name should not be confused with technical definitions. Hence, M does not always mean 'metro' according to the Dutch and French meaning of the word. Often this logo indicates the metropolitan nature of a particular system. M stands for urban in this regard. Another example in German-speaking countries is the famous U–Bahn logo frequently though incorrectly associated with 'underground', while the letter U here stands for the German expression 'Unabhängig', which means independent. Yet another logo with the letter T is used in many cities to symbolize a tram system, however, this is not the case in Stockholm where the metro system is branded with a T derived from 'Tunnelbana', Swedish for metro.

Different types of infrastructures (train, tram, metro), different types of vehicles (e.g., LRV) and related operational, technical and legal features are not relevant for users of public transport. Travelers should only need to understand how the public transport systems work and how they can be used. Therefore a light rail system must be legible. Travellers must easily understand their transport system.

Light rail and other public transport systems perform well only if they are perceived to be coherent and effective (Table 2.6). Light rail being presented convincingly and coherently is therefore very important. Naming and branding help to boost the legibility of light rail systems.

Table 2.6 Legibility: Outline of Relative Levels of Perception

	Light Rail	Regiotram	Tram	Train	Metro
Generic	++	+	+	0	0
In city	+	+	++	−	−

Typology of Urban Rail

	Light rail		Non- light rail
1	Tram *)	6	Train
2	TramTrain	7	Metro
3	TrainTram	8	MetroTrain
4	TramMetro	9	TrainMetro
5	MetroTram		

*) Tram: includes
Urban tram
(traditional, 2ⁿᵈ generation tram, and American streetcar),
Regional tram (sometimes branded as 'regiotram').

A light rail — B non-light rail.

A — Light Rail Operation
Tram/Regiotram (Type 1)

French-style second-generation trams, Dublin, Ireland.

In many European countries modern city trams serve large and medium-sized cities. Some examples from our series of 61 cases are Antwerp (Belgium), Barcelona (Spain), Dublin (Ireland), The Hague (Netherlands), Lyon *Tramway* (France), Nice (France) and Nottingham (UK). Most cities with more than 200,000 inhabitants have a tramway network. Most of these examples are referred to as a 'tram' or 'tramway'. For example 'Strassenbahn' (Germany), 'tranvía' (Spain) or 'spårvagn' (Sweden).

In similar urban situations in America a city tram is called a 'streetcar', while heavier tram vehicles and related infrastructure, including urban-regional systems, are commonly referred to as light rail. In Europe light rail is sometimes literally translated, such as 'tren ligero' (Spain) and 'letbanen' (Denmark). In addition, one can speak of 'Stadtbahn' (Germany) or 'sneltram' (Netherlands).

Continued

Typology of Urban Rail—cont'd
Tram-train (Type 2)

A pioneer tram-train is the famous Karlsruhe system, Germany.

This hybrid form of light rail has a long history, both in Europe and America, where trams drove from the railroad into the built up areas of towns and cities by sharing tracks with local tramways. The technical and functional requirements and conditions for vehicles and infrastructure were still simple and limited at that time.

Currently, the pioneer example is Karlsruhe's light rail system. This system consists of LRVs that run from the urban tramway network onto the heavy rail network where they share tracks with all kinds of trains (both freight and passenger trains, including even the high-speed train ICE). All technical issues, like wheel profile, power supply and security have been adequately solved here due to close cooperation between the tram company, railway company and technical university. Similar examples from Germany can be found in Saarbrücken (one of our cases), Kassel and Chemnitz. In France, such a regional tram-train can be found in the urban region of Mulhouse.

Sometimes tram-train means light rail using former railways, where a classic train service has been removed, and hence, there is no mixed operation in these cases. Examples are our RandstadRail case in the Netherlands and the light rail system in the urban area of Manchester (UK), also one of our cases, where trams run from new tramways in the streets of the city through various adapted railways. In France examples are operational in the Paris metropolis. In the region of Nantes and the case region Lyon (also both in France) tram-train exclusively makes use of the adapted heavy rail infrastructure.

Typology of Urban Rail—cont'd

Train-tram (Type 3)

Train shares tracks and terminus of the local city tram, Zwickau, Germany.

This mode of operation existed a few decades ago in the German city of Cologne, where the *Köln–Bonner Eisenbahn* ran through into the city on the local tramway and mixed with other traffic. In 1999, this hybrid mode was introduced in the German city of Zwickau, in this case with diesel-electric trains and an additional rail to offer standard gauge for trains along the alignment of the narrow-gauge city tram. The most eye-catching challenge was the large size of the train compared to the local trams and other traffic.

No current European example exists of a train-tram using its own dedicated tracks in an urban setting. Only the *EuregioBahn* in Aix-la-Chapelle (Aachen, Germany) considered a plan to extend their trains into the centre of the city, however, this plan was never implemented. In America, such a plan was realized in 2004. Diesel-electric vehicles of the *River Line* run into the town of Camden (New Jersey) near Philadelphia at the other side of the Delaware river. In this town trains run over a considerable length mixed with local road traffic. According to American standards this operation is referred to as light rail. In the past, in America, Switzerland and Japan, there were many examples, some of which still exist, such as *South Shore Line* trains through the streets of Michigan City (Indiana, US), or the *Enoden* system through the city of Enoshima (Japan).

Continued

Typology of Urban Rail—cont'd

Metro-tram (Type 4)

Metro-tram LRV of line 51 in Amstelveen, Amsterdam region, Netherlands.

This hybrid form of light rail has been present since 1990 in the urban area of Amsterdam (Netherlands), where, in the south of the city, in the municipality of Amstelveen, metro line 51 has a joint route with city tram line 5. Challenges included differences in platform height, vehicle width and power supply. Lack of traffic safety at grade intersections was also a problem particularly linked to the larger metro vehicles. It is no surprise this mixed operation will be terminated in a few years and replaced by a new regiotram. Our case *RandstadRail*, also in the Netherlands, represents a second example. On a part of this light rail system, vehicles of the Rotterdam metro share tracks with trams of The Hague.

In the Norwegian capital Oslo, a section of track sharing (between Jar and Bekkestua) was operated until January 2015. Both tram ('trikk') and metro ('T-bane') used the same infrastructure. Malfunctions in the commonly used signal system were the main reason for ending this hybrid system.

In the Netherlands there is also an example without mixed operation: Rotterdam Alexander, where metro on some sections of the network continues on tramway-like infrastructure, including several grade intersections. Like in Amstelveen this caused dangerous situations and serious accidents when the LRV's priority was not recognized by road traffic and pedestrians.

Metro-tram remains, however, mainly a typical Dutch affair, due to historic considerations of introducing classic metro operations in the cities of Rotterdam and Amsterdam, instead of allowing light rail to evolve from existing tramways, i.e., the tram-metro solution, see next section.

Typology of Urban Rail—cont'd
Tram-metro (Type 5)

LRV using metro-style infrastructure and stations, Düsseldorf, Germany.

This metro-style light rail is well-known in Germany, where in many cities urban trams use infrastructure (tunnels, viaducts, stations) according to metro standards, such as Duisburg, Düsseldorf, Cologne, Bonn, Frankfurt, Mülheim, Essen, Bochum, Dortmund, Hannover, Bielefeld and Stuttgart. Only in a few cases was tram-metro converted to full metro, namely in the cities of Frankfurt, Mülheim, Essen, Bochum and Dortmund. But most German tram-metro systems remain in operation. In Cleveland (Ohio, US) there is also a tram-metro. In the centre of this city LRVs share tracks in the metro line tunnel.

Tram-metro is especially considered when a full metro is under construction over a very long period of time. With tram-metro operation, parts of the new infrastructure can be used in advance. The first metro line from Stockholm (Sweden) was established in this way. In Brussels (Belgium), the metro network is being developed in a similar way. However, in Antwerp (also Belgium), full metro won't be an option after all and tram-metro operation has become standard.

B — Non-Light Rail Operation
Train (Type 6)

Regional train at one of the stations in Zug, Switzerland.

Continued

Typology of Urban Rail—cont'd

In the Netherlands, so-called 'Sprinter' trains are accessing and connecting urban regions, including intensive suburban traffic, mainly in the metropolitan area of the Randstad. These heavy rail operations usually involve mixed traffic with intercity trains and freight trains. In Germany, the S-Bahn ('Stadtschnell-Bahn) is well-known. These systems use suburban trains that often drive on separate tracks and, due to their high frequencies and short distances, also take urban-regional transport. In order to improve access to city centres, tunnels and viaducts dedicated for S-Bahn vehicles have been built in various major urban areas. Similar train services are offered in Paris under the name RER (Réseau Express Régional), while in London some suburban trains are interconnected or connected through the city. Elsewhere in Europe, such systems are also present in and around major cities such as Madrid and Barcelona in Spain (Cercanías), Zurich in Switzerland (S-Bahn) and Vienna in Austria (S-Bahn).

In case of modest demand, shorter and lighter trains can provide regional services. An example is the system (branded as 'Stadtbahn') serving the smaller urban region of the city of Zug in Switzerland. In similar regions in Europe, and especially in rural areas, such 'lighter' train systems exist in large numbers, with mostly successful operations.

Japan also hosts many of this kind of train systems, frequently with light rail characteristics. In the United States so-called commuter rail has been implemented in recent years, serving many metropolitan areas. Compared to European and Japanese standards these American systems operate rather heavy trains, for example, in the metropolitan area of Los Angeles, with the commuter train system branded as *Metrolink*.

Metro (Type 7)

The *Muzha-line* on one of the many elevated sections, Taipei, Taiwan.

Typology of Urban Rail—cont'd

The name for 'metro' is derived from the French expression 'métro' which is an abbreviation of 'metropolitan railroad' in late 19th-century Paris. The name has been adopted by various languages worldwide. In American English, however, one speaks of the 'subway'. In addition, the term metro is used very often as a common brand name for an urban public transport system. In Asia the expression 'metro' isn't well-known, contrary to the expression 'MRT', that is, 'mass rapid transit'.

Most European cities with more than 1 million inhabitants have a metro system, but often with different sizes, power supplies and security systems. Some of these metro systems have light rail characteristics, such as the metro in the Dutch city of Rotterdam. American and Asian metro systems usually serve cities with a few million inhabitants or more.

As a special family, the fully automated minimetro must be mentioned, which, in different versions, runs worldwide in many places. The 'Véhicule Automatique Léger' (VAL) is a well-known example of a metro technology developed in France, operating in Lille, Rennes and Toulouse, but also in Turin (Italy) and on the Muzha line in Taipei (Taiwan). The VAL (and similar systems) also operate as a 'people mover system' when they are used to provide shuttle services to airports such as Paris Orly (France) and Chicago O'Hare (Chicago, US).

The metro systems of other cities such as Lausanne (Switzerland) and Copenhagen (Denmark) use technology with similar features. This is also referred to as 'light metro', due to the lighter design requirements for shorter and narrower trains and tighter curves in the tracks. A well-known and very successful example of this is the 'London *Docklands Light Railway*'. In Asia, many metro systems with lighter design requirements, such as sharper horizontal and vertical curves, are often performed with monorail technology.

Metro-train (Type 8)

Metro-train on a classic heavy rail bridge, Newcastle, UK.

Continued

Typology of Urban Rail—cont'd

Metro-train operation implies a metro service through running from its own infrastructure over a traditional railway, hence, track sharing with heavy rail trains, including freight trains. This mix is a technical challenge, partly due to security and platform problems. An old example of a metro-train is the service on the London *Bakerloo line*, which passes from Queen's Park to the suburban railway line to Watford. Another example from London is the service of the *Central line*, that uses shared heavy rail from Stratford to the north-east. Tyneside (Newcastle, UK) hosts a contemporary example, where the metro between Pelow and Sunderland uses a mainline railway.

Train-metro (Type 9)

Meinohama station offers through connection between metro and railway, Fukuoka, Japan.

Train-metro is typically a Japanese invention. For example Tokyo, where some regional trains penetrate the inner city using local metro tunnels. However, the difference between train-metro and metro-train is not always obvious in Japan, since differences between train and metro vehicles are often limited. An example in this regard are the vehicles used for continuous regional operation within the metropolitan area of Fukuoka. Coming from Japanese Rail's *Chikuhi line* infrastructure between Nishi-Karatsu and Meinohama towards the *Kūkō line* of Fukuoka's metro system.

Urban Regional Heavy Rail

Dutch regional heavy rail train at one of its new stations (Amsterdam region, Netherlands).

Many urban regions in Europe and Asia, and to some extent also in the US, are also operated by heavy rail. These regional trains often offer good connections in these regions (and beyond). The accessibility of local destinations, however, is a less powerful achievement of such systems. Where with light rail on parts of a line, some relatively short stops provide short walking and cycling distances, in a heavy rail scenario, only one station is available, with obviously much larger distances for walking, cycling or driving. The final part of the journey will be longer.

In the Netherlands, the number of regional stations along main heavy rail lines has been significantly expanded in recent years, sometimes in combination with property development. One of the many examples is the station at Halfweg-Zwanenburg in the urban region of Amsterdam.

Bus Rapid Transit

Bogota hosts a huge BRT-network. It is a true showcase in South America, despite being heavily overused.

To a certain extent, the performance of light rail can be matched, or at least approached, with high-quality urban-regional bus networks. In America the heavy version of such systems is referred to as 'bus rapid transit' (BRT). BRT is especially applied in South American countries in situations where light rail and metro would certainly be justified.

The high quality of BRT is inextricably linked to a heavy infrastructure: an almost completely free bus alignment with occasionally grade intersections, with station-like stops.

Formally known as *Zuidtangent*, the BRT system in the Amsterdam region proved to be highly successful. (*Image by Kees Pronk.*)

Bus Rapid Transit—cont'd

The BRT in Bangkok has been subject to controversies as owners of cars and mopeds didn't like the loss of one of their traffic lanes when the new bus service was introduced.

Applications can also be found in Europe and Asia, such as parts of the regional bus system around Amsterdam (Netherlands) that easily meets heavy BRT criteria. The same applies, for example, to the BRT line in Bangkok, which in part has its own heavy infrastructure.

Many high-quality bus systems in European cities are more likely to meet the French criteria of 'bus à haut niveau de service' (BHNS), i.e., a bus with a high level of service quality. A nice example of BHNS is *Le Busway* in Nantes, which demonstrates how bus and light rail can be integrated into an efficient public transport network.

Cohesion of space and mobility (e.g., transit oriented development) can be supported with high-quality bus systems. But where sustainable infrastructure is lacking, as most often in (historic) city centres, this cohesion is not guaranteed for a longer period of time.

Light rail returned in Stockholm. The new system is extended constantly and combines tram, metro and train characteristics.

CHAPTER 3

Light Rail Returns

One of our cases: the new urban tramway (left) and airport express train (right; in red livery) in Lyon, France (2013).

Again, one of our cases: the new light rail in Portland, Oregon, also entails an airport line (Beaverton, 2012). *(Image by Bas Govers.)*

Light Rail Transit Systems
ISBN 978-0-12-814784-9
https://doi.org/10.1016/B978-0-12-814784-9.00003-7

After decades of decline, rail infrastructure has returned to European and North American cities since the late 1970s. In Europe, existing tram systems have been expanded, and in many other cities and urban areas, tramways have been rebuilt. In North America, light rail has been introduced in many cities, and is increasingly complemented by 'lighter' tramways, called 'streetcars'.

In Europe and North America, many regional railways have been operated in a new way, sometimes after years of shutdown. Of course, new urban metro systems should be mentioned here too, together with high-speed trains connecting many of the new light rail cities. In addition, metro, high-speed railways and light rail systems have been introduced in Asia.

This renewed orientation of urban development on high-quality public transport has been part of the urban development of the last few decades. It is therefore not surprising that there is an increasing interest in transit oriented development (TOD). Against the historical background of urban developments in the late 19th and early 20th centuries, the revival of public transport in the 1970s could be seen as a prologue to a revolution that led to TOD.

3.1 LIGHT RAIL AND TOD AVANT LA LETTRE

Light rail avant la lettre in The Hague Region, Netherlands (Leidschendam, October 13, 1961). *(Image by L.J.P. Albers.)*

The development of modern cities would have been unthinkable without 'transit' (i.e., urban mass transport with tramways and urban railways). Cities could only grow at their unprecedented rate in the course of the 19th century thanks to the invention of urban public transport by rail. It was initially the new (horse and steam) tramways that carried urban development and thus they should be considered as precursors to current light rail systems. These first tram systems were later expanded into large, often regional networks operated with express trams, such as the extensive network of blue trams in the urban regions of Lyon (France) with its Train Bleu, the Netherlands with its 'Blue Trams', and the 'Pacific Electric' with its 'Red Cars' in Greater Los Angeles. When cities like Paris reached a metropolitan size, the 'metropolitan' railways gave way to a new form of transit, which is often referred to with the originally French word 'métro'.

This rail-oriented urban development was typical for Europe and America. For example, in many European and American cities, such as Los Angeles, in the early 20th century, private rail companies and real estate developers built urban and regional tramways, mostly along newly con-structed tracks that often determine the urban street pattern to this day. The land purchased by private developers along the tramways created was profitably developed with housing and related facilities, or sold with profit to other commercial parties. In this way, urbanization accelerated throughout Europe and America.

In the 1950s, car traffic increased significantly throughout Europe and public transport's share decreased. In North America, this has already started in the 1930s. In South America, almost all rail systems were abolished, not just city trams, but also many railways. The link between urban develop-ment and transit seemed to disappear forever. In countries like France and Spain, for example, almost all tram systems were dismantled.

As for TOD, the abolishment of regional rail systems was particularly disastrous. For example, in the early 1960s, all of the previously mentioned 'blue trams' in the urban areas of the Netherlands and Lyon (France) were eliminated, and the same thing happened with the last Red Cars in Los Angeles. Two exceptions should, however, be mentioned, Switzerland and Japan. In both these countries the operation of regional light and heavy railway systems was continued.

Symbolic for the decoupling of urban development and public trans-port, and even of transport in general, is the unfortunate relationship be-tween urbanization and the development of highways through or along existing cities and their suburbs. Urban planning and traffic planning were at odds. Usually car traffic got priority. Urban areas extensively made way for motorways. The importance of 'transit' was completely underestimated. In North America, cities transformed into a kind of amorphous 'sprawl', while at the same time depopulating inner cities lost their main functions.

As a counter reaction, more and more activists opposed the unilateral approach to urban mobility. Journalist and author Jane Jacobs (1916−2006) protested, with her actions and her books, against the megalomaniac motorway plans in Manhattan from the notorious city planner Robert Moses (1888−1981). Similar protests were taking place in Europe against the same kind of plans. However, rail-bound public transport never completely disappeared, not even in 'car country' Germany. Also, tramways were retained in most major cities of Austria, Belgium, Italy, the Netherlands and Switzerland (and throughout Eastern Europe).

A turnaround took place in several cities when the construction of metro systems started in the late 1960s and early 1970s, and the importance of travelling by train became clear again. In the Netherlands, the services on the existing heavy rail network were enhanced and a 'clock fixed' timetable was introduced in combination with reliable train interconnections at dedicated nodes. This revolutionary approach was copied and improved by the Swiss railways.

In addition, new suburbs in several European countries got local and regional stops at the existing heavy rail network, with which for the first time a link between urban development and transit was established. For the same reason, the remaining tram networks of many cities were expanded to connect new suburbs.

From that time came the famous Dutch 'ABC policy' that entailed so-called A-sites proposed at main railway station nodes without necessarily car-access. These sites prevailed over fully car-oriented C-sites at urban fringes, or B-sites in between served by local—regional public transport as well as roads. Despite the overwhelming attention of politicians and professionals in other countries this ABC policy didn't became successful. After all, despite ABC aims, at the very same time new highways were planned and constructed that boosted development of C- instead of A-sites!

Nevertheless, new tramways in countries like Germany and the Netherlands marked a transition in thinking about mobility. Time became ripe for the return of light rail. After all, the A-sites in Dutch cities can't be viewed other than a kind of TOD avant la lettre. The renewed attention for the relationship between rail and urban development shows that light rail is important for the desired direction of this development, such as concentrations at public transport nodes.

Besides development of Dutch A-sites or Swiss nodes, TOD avant la lettre unfolded in a second form. Various countries created with their new urban planning policies and related logistic and economic considerations so-called 'new towns' that were a substantial distance (15—35 km) from their 'mother cities'. For instance, in the late 1970s in the Paris metropolitan region five new towns ('villes nouvelles') were planned and eventually constructed. In the same period in the Netherlands many cities were completed with similar new towns, called 'growth cores'('groeikernen').

All those new towns required new connections with the main city centre and important urban centres. For this reason in Paris the RER ('*Réseau Express Régional*') was created, a regional heavy rail system compiled from partly new suburb—city centre underground lines and adapted commuter rail lines. In the Netherlands some new towns got new regional train connections, like Zoetermeer ('*Sweet Lake City*'), in the urban region of The Hague and Almere and Lelystad in the Amsterdam metropolitan area, while other new towns got improved regional services on existing main lines. At that time in the urban region of Rotterdam (also in the Netherlands) the metro (opened in 1968) was extended in two stages (1974, 1985) along the former route of the regional tramway (closed in 1965) to serve a new town southwest of the city.

The new light rail system in new town Tuen Mun in the metropolitan area of Hong Kong (2011).

Light rail definitively returned around 1980 when France, Germany and the Netherlands started constructing and preparing new systems and North America entered its new transit epoch with the opening of the very first series of new light rail systems in Edmonton (Alberta, Canada, 1978 — our case), Calgary (Alberta, Canada, 1981) and San Diego (US, California, 1981). Africa got a new light rail system in Tunis (1985), and Asia followed with a new light rail system in the new town Tuen Mun (1988) in the metropolitan area of Hong Kong.

Some European projects, in particular, set the stage for light rail. German industry had already invented its famous *U2* light rail vehicle for the city of Frankfurt (1968) and additionally an impressive series of systems served with so-called '*Stadtbahn B*' vehicles defined light rail standards during the mid-1970s and early 1980s in the urban regions of the Ruhr area and Cologne–Bonn.

In the Dutch urban region of Utrecht a new light rail system (selected as one of our cases) was introduced in 1983 (and extend in stages). Denoted as 'rapid tramway' ('*sneltram*') it served two new towns. Two years later the city of Nantes (France) opened its new tram system as the first of a new generation of urban light rail in France. A further two years later (1987) the city of Grenoble followed with its cutting-edge system. Ever since the tram in France has been an integral part of urban development, urban renewal and revitalization of cities. The French tramways became a success formula that is still copied in cities around the world.

From Pacific Electric to Metro Los Angeles

In the early 20th century, Los Angeles hosted a very extensive light rail system. The 'Pacific Electric' accessed with its renowned 'Red Cars' a metropolitan area that extended beyond more than 50 miles from downtown. This early example of a true light rail system served dozens of 'incorporated' cities like San Fernando, Hollywood, Pasadena, San Bernardino and Orange, but also coastal places like Newport Beach, Long Beach, San Pedro and Santa Monica. In its peak days the Pacific Electric network measured more than 1600 km.

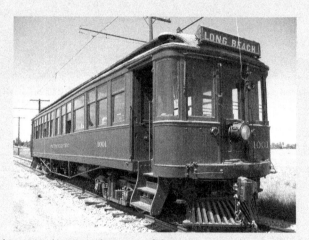

Delivered in 1913 the interurban cars of the 1000 class were the first big cars to be ordered by Pacific Electric's new management. PE car 1001 has been preserved. *(Image by Oleknutlee.)*

From Pacific Electric to Metro Los Angeles—cont'd

Los Angeles owns a cutting edge light rail system, called Metro. Light rail returned to this metropolis at Long Beach (2007).

Like almost all other urban rail systems in the United States, Los Angeles's light rail disappeared in less than 30 years. The last line, between downtown and the port city of Long Beach, was closed in 1961. However, from the late 1980s, light rail returned to Los Angeles. It is no coincidence that the first new line, the Blue Line (opened in 1990), coincides almost entirely with the old Long Beach line under the brand name 'Metro'. Ever since a high-quality public transport system has been developed, beside the light rail are a high-quality bus (BRT, 'bus rapid transit') and regional rail services (commuter rail).

The Los Angeles case illustrates how much urban planning and mobility are related. Unlike the common view, Los Angeles appears both in the past and nowadays not to be a car city, but a rail city — that is, a transit city, whose average urban density is now the highest of all cities in the United States.

3.2 STADTBAHN MEANS LIGHT RAIL IN GERMANY

Germany has had a long rail history and, since the 1970s, new forms of urban and urban—regional rail public transport have been developed. Since many German cities were deemed somewhat too small for an actual underground railway (metro) a lighter hybrid form was introduced (like in the Ruhr region, in the vast region of Karlsruhe, but also in cities like Frankfurt and Cologne, which happen to be similar to the Dutch cities of Amsterdam and Rotterdam in terms of size and density). The *Stadtbahn* (literally 'city rail', or, in other words, light rail) was specifically used to connect and open up existing and new regional–urban centres. This is a German form of TOD, although the abbreviation TOD is not used because of the German meaning of the word ('death').

The *Stadtbahn* vehicles turned out to be successful German export products for the American market. Though the Canadian cities of Edmonton (our case) and Calgary had preceded it, the first light rail system in the United States was introduced in San Diego in 1981. This system was operated using bright red light rail vehicles based on the U2 LRV design from Frankfurt. San Diego was obviously inspired by our Canadian Edmonton case, because the German U2s had been driving there since the system opened in 1978. The term TOD started being used more and more frequently in the years to follow and is practically always connected to the, also American, term 'light rail'. Strictly speaking, this can be considered a German, or possibly European, invention that found its way back to the old continent due to an American U-turn. It would not be bad to keep the European/German origins of TOD in mind. It is thought to be an exclusively American invention only too often, and its implementations are generally accepted without any critical thought. It would be good if suitable examples were looked for in countries like the Netherlands, Denmark, France and Germany.

The latter brings our brief history to a point where TOD can be defined more precisely. The moment that more interest is paid to rail-based public transport is the moment when it is possible to have this form of public transport affecting urban development. Bearing this in mind, TOD is nothing less and nothing more than bringing the urban development into the proximity of new or existing public transport lines. History justifies this definition, since it reflects the way urbanization started in the mid-19th century. This is the reason why since the 1990s urban development has been centred around the main stations in the Netherlands, but in other European countries, too.

If TOD is considered an American term, then a stricter definition is justified. In this case the term stands for regional urban development near new regional light rail lines and their stops in particular. The corresponding development, differentiated according to multilevel typology and the corresponding programmes, is as follows:

- The main stop is in the city centre (usually a group of stops close together and integrated in public space) and serves highly urban programmes.

- In addition to this there are stops at so-called regional centres, or regional hubs, which provide regional shopping facilities or offices and/or housing in, to American standards, high density. Other important stops serve educational and medical facilities.
- Finally there are 'transit centres', which are hubs that facilitate changing to a different mode of public transport (e.g., local bus lines) and cars. Urban development around these kinds of stops is possible, but in general is not essential. A simple variety is the 'park and ride' (P&R) stop, which tends to be positioned where a railway terminates. This position allows light rail to drastically increase its range in and beyond the original region (an essential characteristic of light rail and TOD in America).

Our Portland (Oregon, US) case is generally considered as a perfect example of TOD based on a regional light rail network. In Europe this could be the Stuttgart (Germany) urban region, or our Manchester (UK) case with the regional *Metrolink* system. Many cities in America have now followed examples like these, and other countries have adopted the TOD formula too, as can be concluded from our case examples from Europe and elsewhere.

Development of urban concentration around light rail and heavy rail stations and stops has soared in Asia. Japan, with its metropolitan, highly dense development and extensive rail networks, has undeniably set a trend. The practice in Japan with its heavily developed station surroundings has taught us that the main purpose of TOD is to concentrate destinations (work, education, retail) as much as possible around stations and main stops.

Portland: Light Rail Implies Urban Planning

Portland, Oregon, is known as the most advanced city in the field of high-quality urban planning and high-quality public transport. The city and its region are also a breeding ground for TOD. In recent years, this concept has been further developed in the Streetcar project: the tramway as a form of urban planning.

Portland's innovations in urban planning and transport date back to the early 1970s when the urban crisis in America was at its peak. Throughout the country, residents moved away from inner cities. Economic activities in the city centres stopped and the centres were extinct and decayed. In those days, cities were compared to doughnuts, empty on the inside and expanding on the outside. The explosively increasing car traffic deteriorated the quality of the urban environment.

Continued

Portland: Light Rail Implies Urban Planning—cont'd

Portland was the first city to change its ways. First, a new park was developed on the banks of the Willamette River, which flows through the city centre. The park replaced a highway that was demolished for this purpose. It was a true revolution. Plans for a new highway through the city were also cancelled. At the same time, a regional transport authority was set up to develop plans for a regional light rail system.

Under the name of MAX (Metropolitan Area Express), the first line of this light rail system opened in 1987. Later, more lines followed. MAX now serves a large part of Portland's urban region. It is the infrastructural backbone of 'Metro 2040', the regional plan that provides for the development of the greater city. The 'TOD principle' forms the basis of the plan, because urban development is concentrated in the urban regions around the MAX stops. The inner city is the core of this light rail network.

With the success of MAX, the city centre was revitalized. Roads were narrowed and the number of parking spaces was reduced. Public space is becoming more important. Urbanization improves this public space. Portland is blessed with small blocks. Its typical fine-grained grid structure implies relatively large block front length, hence, there are opportunities to access apartments, amenities and other urban functions within the blocks from the public realm.

Streetcar as a selling point for real estate, Portland, Pearl District (2004).

The Streetcar project is the closing piece of Portland's urban renewal. The first stage of this city tramway was opened in 2001, offering excellent accessibility to the Pearl District as a new high-quality residential area.

Portland: Light Rail Implies Urban Planning—cont'd

Portland Streetcar is owned by the City of Portland. Portland Streetcar Inc. (PSI) is a nonprofit organization responsible for the maintenance, operation and construction of streetcar extensions. Citizens and other stakeholders, including shopkeepers and property owners, take part in the PSI board. The municipality is responsible for the operating costs. Entrepreneurs in the city have incurred some of the building costs. In addition, there are revenues from land sales and local taxes, such as higher parking fees. Project developers along the line have a relatively high degree of freedom to complete their projects.

Pearl District represents urban renewal centred around a new streetcar line (tramway). The Aerial view shows the well-developed urban situation (December 2017). *(Image by Martin Glastra van Loon.)*

Continued

Portland: Light Rail Implies Urban Planning—cont'd

Already during the first years of the project, a lot of investment has been done in property, real estate and facilities: in housing, offices and amenities such as a hotel and many shops. New urban developments have been concentrated successfully with the block adjacent to the tramway. Less than 10 years after the first tram route was established in 1997, more than half of all urban development was taking place here. In the years afterwards tram and light rail were expanded much further, again in conjunction with urban investment.

3.3 LIGHT RAIL AND TOD IN EUROPE AND ELSEWHERE

In hindsight, the revival of public transport in the 1970s can be seen as the prologue to the past three decades, which has been a period of increased high-quality public transport and new possibilities for TOD. To illustrate this development we will describe proceedings from the European cities of Utrecht (the Netherlands) and Strasbourg (France). Finally, we will look at the rest of the world where recent developments have been strongly influenced by European technologies and experiences.

New regiotram, or 'express tram' ('*Sneltram*') in Utrecht: pioneer light rail project in the Netherlands.

The Utrech *SUNIJ* light rail — *Sneltram* ('express tram') — represents beyond any doubt the first European example of a completely new light rail system (1983), which was modelled after the American (actually German) system. The Utrecht *Sneltram* to the 'new towns' of Nieuwegein and IJsselstein to the south of the city can be compared to its North American and German counterparts, both technically (vehicles, infrastructure) and spatially (regional range, serving regional centres and residential areas).

Nevertheless, this Dutch example stands out from its counterparts. Utrecht currently lacks an important TOD characteristic: light rail lines are supposed to continue all the way into the city centre, in order for regional centres to be connected to the main centre and to open up the main centre by including centre stops. This project involves only two stops at the end of the line near Utrecht Central Station, therefore serving only a part of the city centre.

The next project in Utrecht (our second case) was aimed at continuing a new tramway through the city centre to the other side of the urban region in order to be able to offer a regional diametric line and the urban developments to go with it. The final destination of the intended line was the university area of the Uithof in the east of the city. This project has faced difficulties in planning from the outset. Residents and shopkeepers, who feared traffic would become more dangerous, constantly and powerfully opposed the plans. Opposition was caused mainly because the intended tram, whose vehicles would look a lot like those of the then-new French trams in places like Grenoble (see our Strasbourg case further on) were considered similar to the existing quite 'heavy' regional light rail (see our first case above). The tram project was part of TOD that oversaw the redevelopment of Utrecht Central Station, which also faced a lot of opposition. An underground tram station was part of this project. The national central government also opposed the tram project because of the high costs.

Many other factors made it extremely difficult to realize the tram project. These factors included political instability, unclear decision making, an antitram lobby active in the background and fed by populist politicians, and the opposition of the former director of the municipal bus company at the time. Finally the plan was cancelled after the 1995 municipal elections and the subsequent change of power. Several conversations with people who were involved at the time have led to the conclusion that the project would have been likely to succeed if it had been concluded some weeks before the municipal elections, instead of just after, even though the national government would have been the one to finance it (though later this proved to be doubtful). However, in place of the tram project a bus project was started, which resulted in a high-quality bus line along the alignment of the intended tram route. The busway was initially intended to be able to be converted into a tramway, enabling long-term rail-based TOD.

A major public action in the planning process for the new tramway in Utrecht was showcase test runs on the old *SUNIJ* light rail line with a state-of-the-art low-floor tram rented from Mulhouse, France (September 2007).

Our next case is the *Uithof line*, the third Utrecht tram project. This concerns a new tramway, again to the university area of the Uithof, only this time around the city centre, instead of through it. Over the past few years different parts of this project, like the substructure and a stop that is shared with the new Vaartsche Rijn regional train station, have slowly and incrementally, but steadily, been built. An important activity for the public was implementing test rides on the old line with a state-of-the-art low-floor tram which had been rented from the new tram company of Mulhouse, France (September 2007). The project is to facilitate the essential, but overcrowded connection between the Utrecht Central Station and the university area. A new park and ride facility at the end of the line has also been incorporated into this project. In this way the project solves some shortcomings of the present system and the TOD potential of the university area is utilized.

A strong point is the new Vaartsche Rijn regional train station where passengers can change to the new *Uithof line*. The station is part of the *RandstadSpoor* project, which provides a regional train system (heavy rail) using the *Sprinter* formula of the Dutch Railways (NS). The tramway will open in 2019.

The new tramway in Strasbourg (France) successfully accesses the city centre (2004).

It is remarkable that around the same time the new tramway in Strasbourg (*Ligne A*) opened (1994) a similar project in Utrecht was about to fail (1995). This is all the more remarkable since both cities and their urban regions are very much alike in terms of size (surface area as well as number of inhabitants). Strasbourg was not the first second-generation tram system in France. This was Nantes (1985), followed by Grenoble (1987) and then by our French case Paris *T1* (1992). Still, it was going to be the Strasbourg tram that would turn out to be an iconic tram system that convincingly shows that investing in the city pays off. The economic effects of the tram on the city centre are evident.

Like its predecessor in Nantes, the new Strasbourg tramway resulted from a 1973 letter written by Marcel Cavaillé, who was the Junior Cabinet Minister at the time, to the mayors of eight French cities. The immediate cause for this important letter was the global oil crisis and, therefore, the idea that urban transport needed revision. Nantes was the first city that accepted the offer to initiate a tram project that would largely be paid for by the central government. Strasbourg followed many years later, after a long and difficult process of decision making.

In 1985 the board of the urban region (*Communauté Urbaine de Strasbourg*, CUS) chose a *VAL* metro (*Véhicule Automatique Léger*) like the one in Lille. However, this plan was put aside in 1989 after an intense dispute between those in favour and those against. Catherine Trautmann, passionate mayor and also chairwoman of the CUS, decided in favour of the tram.

Strasbourg represents nearly perfectly the new French tram town: a city in which investments in tram infrastructure and urban programmes (retail and property development) are in harmony, which is the core of TOD. The city set the tone with its beautifully designed tram that has low floors over its entire length (*Eurotram*); its predecessors in Nantes and Grenoble were only partially low-floored. The network of our Strasbourg case has by now turned into an extensive network and it is remarkable that a similar city like Utrecht in the Netherlands (see our previous case) managed to remain so far behind. After all those years there is still no tram in Utrecht city centre. Several extensions to the network will be added over the next few years, including the already opened tramway (2017) crossing the border to Kehl in Germany. The main goal of this new international tramway is to facilitate urban redevelopment in the shared harbour area. In spite of all this, Strasbourg, too, has had its setbacks: a project concerning the regional tram-train Strasbourg—Bruche—Piémont des Vosges was put on hold in 2013 due to high costs.

Tramway *T4* in Lyon (France) opened in 2009 and serves precinct États-Unis, according to the famous urban plan of the visionary architect Tony Garnier. In his plan of 1934 the tramway was already projected.

Strasbourg set the tone for many other French cities with similar TOD, including our Nice (2007) and Reims (2011) cases, although the latter already had tram plans before then. Our case of the Lyon urban tram (*Tramway*, 2001) also needs to be noted, since it completes the existing metro network. Still, the new tram has turned out to be important enough for a role in TOD: tramway *T4*, which opened in 2009 (Lyon, France), serves the États-Unis neighbourhood, which is in accordance with the plans of the visionary architect Tony Garnier. These plans that date back to 1934 had already included a tramway.

The French model has been applied by many other cities in different countries, including Spain with our Barcelona case (2004) and Zaragoza (2011; using vehicles by Spanish manufacturer CAF). The rest of the world also follows the European tram trend. Jerusalem (2011; our Israel case) has copied the French city tram. Several northern African cities have done the same thing; these cities include Rabat (2011) and our Casablanca case (2012) in Morocco, as well as Algiers (2011) and Constantine (2013) in Algeria. The city of Tunis in Tunisia had a light rail system with vehicles and technologies from Europe modelled after those by the tram company of Hanover in Germany as far back as 1985. Casablanca is our first case in Africa and it shows state-of-the-art technology and knowledge from France. It is an excellent example of French-style TOD.

The first 'French' tram system in South America was adopted in Rio de Janeiro, Brazil (2016), and is our case from that part of the world. The tram (*VLT Carioca*; *Veiculos Leves sobre Trilhos*) will be operated by the French company *RATP DEV* for 25 years. The vehicles, too, are of French origin: the first five low-floor trams (of the *Citadis* type) were manufactured by Alstom in La Rochelle (France); the rest of them in the new Brazilian Alstom factory in Taubaté which opened in 2015. The trams make use of a technology that provides ground-level power supply along the entire route, instead of being powered by traditional overhead lines. The former power supply is of the *Alimentation par le Sol* (APS) type developed by Alstom and first applied in Bordeaux (France). Other South American cities have planned for similar tram systems with European technologies, e.g., the entirely 'French' Alstom project for a new tram in Cuenca (Ecuador). In addition to this, the Argentinian city of Mendoza has had a light rail system (*Metrotranvía*) since 2012, using second-hand vehicles from San Diego (US), manufactured in Germany, originally modelled after the German *U2* cars from Frankfurt. TOD plays a modest role in all these South American projects, though it is clear that trams offer necessary support to the urban development. Realization of the Rio de Janeiro tram project, for instance, would have been unthinkable if it had not been for the Olympic Games in the city.

The European influence also applies to Asia where light rail has made an unprecedented march. The new tram system in Kaohsiung (one of our cases) is a good example of TOD and the latest tram technologies from Europe. The same goes for another case from Asia, the Japanese city of Toyama, the showcase light rail of Japan. Various new tram systems in China also use European technology. For instance, the future tram system in the Songjiang suburb of Shanghai (2017) will be supplied with French-style trams of the type *Citadis*. Meanwhile Suzhou (2014) runs with vehicles based on Bombardier's *Flexity 2* design, while the trams in Guangzhou (2014) use various components supplied by Siemens.

The new tramway in Zhuhai (China, 2015) is the first Chinese light rail system equipped with *TramWave*, Ansaldo STS's catenary-free energy supply system. 'A tram arrived at Zhuhai No.1 High School Station'. *(Image by JULIANISME.)*

For our first case in China, the city of Zhuhai (2015), AnsaldoBreda (in co-operation with CNR Dalian) provided Italian-designed Sirio trams. Moreover the tram system is equipped with the *TramWave* catenary-free electrification system developed by Ansaldo STS. TOD characteristics of these new Chinese tram cities are weak, despite European involvement. Predominantly the tramways are complementary to existing metro systems, or serve rather new, though already existing, housing developments. However, our preliminary case study of Zhuhai's tram proved this new light rail system represents a new and independent system. The first line is largely situated along an existing main road serving new and existing properties. Aesthetics or urban planning considerations played a role, for instance in the eye-catching design of the tram stops, however, catenary-free operation was specified because of the high incidence of typhoons. Indeed, 'TOD characteristics' are weak, but present. During 2016 the system unfortunately still suffered technical problems.

The European influence is also obvious in our two cases in Australia. The new light rail system in Queensland, known as *Gold Coast Light Rail* (2014), runs with *Flexity 2* trams built by Bombardier in Germany, while the system is operated by the French firm Keolis in a joint venture with the Australian company Downer Rail. Gold Coast Light Rail successfully connects a string of high-density coastal centres, hence, TOD has been optimized.

Since 2014 services on the *Inner West Light Rail* of Sydney (1997) have been provided by a fleet of *Urbos 3* trams designed and built by the Spanish company CAF (replacing the old fleet of German-designed vehicles). For the new *CBD and South East Light Rail*, due to open in 2019, the French company Alstom will supply *Citadis X05* trams. 'TOD characteristics' of the future two-line network are strong as waterfront and central business district (re)developments are served very well.

Originally centred in Europe and North America light rail combined with TOD has spread elsewhere in the world. Next to Africa, South America, the Far East and Australia, the Middle East should also be mentioned with a new system in Dubai, UAE, (2014) served by state-of-the-art facilities, 100% APS ground-level power supply and low-floor Citadis trams, both delivered by the French company Alstom. The first stage of the line in the Marina district already features TOD.

With European involvement and support, at least three new light rail systems in the Middle East will be installed in the years to come: Abu Dhabi (UAE), Doha (Qatar) and Lusail (Qatar). Though not one of our case studies, the latter is a nice example of TOD since it was constructed mutually with the development of this new town.

For completeness, our case of the proposed new light rail system in Almaty, Kazakhstan (former Soviet Union), should be mentioned. Preliminary preparations and investigations for the envisaged project included Western support. As a matter of fact, the system will be constructed on the remains of parts of the former tramway system (finally closed in 2015). TOD is part of the first stage of the project that incorporates a connection from the centre to new developments in the western part of the city.

Edmonton (Canada) Marks Return of Light Rail

Siemens LRVs of Edmonton Transit System (ETS). *(Image by Axel Kuehn.)*

Edmonton (Alberta) represents the pioneer light rail project in Canada, being the first light rail project of its kind in North America (April 1978). The new system features TOD. Edmonton also made us aware of the historic roots of urban planning and rail-based public transport (e.g., streetcar in the US).

Between the 1930s and 1960s nearly all light rail systems (streetcar, interurban) in North America were wiped out. Only a few systems survived, e.g., Boston (Massachusetts), Cleveland (Ohio), New Orleans (Louisiana), Newark (New Jersey), Philadelphia (Pennsylvania), Pittsburgh (Pennsylvania), San Francisco (California) and Toronto (Ontario, Canada). This unprecedented destruction of public transport is often designated as the 'transit holocaust', or the 'transportation conspiracy'. The latter refers to an automobile industry that seems to have deliberately bought and subsequently dismantled rail-based public transport in order to sell their buses and other car products. In fact, several more factors played a role here too: congestion due to increasing car traffic, the rise of the car mobility culture and particularly the lack of required investments. These investments were crucial for the new technical and economic life cycle of the next generation of tramways in American cities — despite the fact that the rail industry between the 1930s and 1960s massively produced and delivered modern PCC cars (named after the 'Presidents' Conference Committee') (1929), which was responsible for the prototype design of this revolutionary vehicle that, in adapted form, has operated in dozens of cities worldwide. However, the private–public transport companies were reluctant to make the required investments, while the

Edmonton (Canada) Marks Return of Light Rail—cont'd

state ideology at that time impeded public investment for such purposes. All these factors were decisive in the decisions to abandon tram systems. Edmonton was no exception and lost its streetcar in 1951.

After four years of construction, Edmonton opened the first stage of its new light rail system on April 22, 1978. Light rail returned, and Edmonton was followed in 1981 by the neighbouring city Calgary (Alberta), and San Diego (California) — the first new light rail city in the US. All these new-generation systems were operated by so-called 'U2' high-floor LRVs, according to the design of ditto cars in Frankfurt, Germany. Obviously, German design and technology played a key role here. For that matter, it is remarkable that some of the U2 cars from San Diego recently have been given a second life on the new light rail system- *Metrotranvía* (2012) in Mendoza, Argentina.

The central portion of the line in Edmonton (with six stations) is underground, including a dedicated bridge over the Saskatchewan river. All other alignments are at grade, though without street running. A second batch of LRVs, type Siemens SD-160, has been introduced since 2008. A second line to the north opened in 2015. New extensions to the west and south-east are in planning, including the use of new low-floor LRVs.

Four coupled Siemens LRVs crossing the Saskatchewan river. *(Image by Axel Kuehn.)*

Historic research has shown the importance of the former streetcar system for urban development and structuring. Symbolic in this regard was the opening in 1980 of the vintage streetcar service of the 'Edmonton Radial

Continued

Edmonton (Canada) Marks Return of Light Rail—cont'd

Railway Society' over the famous High Level Bridge route crossing the Saskatchewan river (parallel to the lower new light rail bridge). TOD in the early days of the city is reflected in the fact that many of the vibrant streets and avenues of today were once the arteries served by streetcar (similar patterns are noticed in our cases of Los Angeles, California and Portland, Oregon). Today in Edmonton, TOD is knowingly part of urban planning and property development policies along both existing and planned light rail lines.

Metrolink of Manchester (UK) Inspires Many Cities

The accessibility of Manchester's city centre has been improved substantially by the new light rail service. Since May 2014 all services have been run by type 'M5000' high-floor LRVs built by Bombardier. Greater Manchester's Metrolink tram number 3009A, in Salford Quays, Greater Manchester, England. *(Image by Tom Page.)*

Manchester's *Metrolink* is the largest light rail system in England. It represents a strong case of successful commercial property development in combination with a new tramway. Manchester especially embodies the return of light rail to the UK. Its system also mirrors all of our Utrecht cases in the Netherlands.

The opening of the new light rail system in Manchester's urban region in 1992 marked the UK's redevelopment outside of London of high-quality public

Metrolink of Manchester (UK) Inspires Many Cities—cont'd

transport, including opportunities for TOD. Similarly to the light rail in Utrecht 10 years earlier in the Netherlands, Manchester represents the first English example of an American/German-inspired light rail system (the previously opened Docklands Light Railway in London is, according to our definition, not a form of light rail). However, unlike in Utrecht, the LRVs in Manchester run from the region into the inner city, in order to connect the regional centres directly with the city centre, including improved accessibility in the centre by means of a few tramway-like stops. For this reason, pragmatically existing regional railways were adapted for light rail operation. With a new tramway through the city centre these former railways were interconnected.

At the end of the 1990s, the branch line through Salford Quays towards Eccles was realized. This new street-based tramway was then explicitly applied for TOD. At the same time, the former port area of the Salford Quays was redeveloped. Different stops offered direct access to new retail outlets, offices and housing. Unfortunately, the tramway was designed with many curves, hence, the LRVs were constrained to rather low speeds. Nevertheless, Metrolink smoothly delivers customers due to its fast connections to various places in the urban region. In 2010 the situation was enhanced with the opening of the MediaCityUK spur.

Manchester's Eccles light rail line has had a noticeable effect on the development and image of the Salford Quays. Integration in the urban environment is remarkable. The distance between the tramway and buildings is particularly small in some respects. In any case, the identity appears to be helpful, so much so that Metrolink is pictured on postcards.

In recent years, the system has been significantly expanded. The so-called Big Bang (2009—17) marked the opening of a second cross-city line (2CC) and a series of new lines into the region connecting places like Rochdale, Ashton, East Didsbury and the local airport with the heart of Manchester city. Work is still underway and planned for new connections, including a line to the Trafford Centre. Metrolink, as a large regional light rail network, can therefore serve as an inspiration for Utrecht in the Netherlands (and similar cities around the world). From the start of the development of this British light rail system improved accessibility of the city centre has been an important precondition. Such access is still lacking in Utrecht's centre. For the future of Utrecht after the opening of its *Uithof line* light rail system in 2019 (one of our cases), Manchester is certainly inspirational.

One final note. Potentially, urban regions of cities like Manchester and Utrecht could benefit from a tram-train. This form of light rail in principle allows vast expansion of today's light rail systems. Whether this will happen in the UK depends on the eventual success of the delayed British tram-train pilot project Sheffield—Rotherham, hopefully due to open in 2018.

RandstadRail (Netherlands): Our Main Showcase Light Rail

An LRV from the Hague network on the common route with Rotterdam line E over the former railway at Leidschenveen station.

RandstadRail in the metropolitan region of The Hague/Rotterdam, Netherlands, is the largest light rail system of the Netherlands and one of our three main cases. This new system marks the return of large-scale light rail after the final withdrawal in 1961 of the former interurban-style system in the region of The Hague.

RandstadRail is made up of two networks that overlap on a section of the former Hofplein railway line between The Hague and Rotterdam (from 1908) and the former railway line to New Town Zoetermeer (from 1977). Two tramway lines have been extended from the city of The Hague to Zoetermeer via the former railway line (with a new route to the new Oosterheem precinct) – operated by low-floor LRVs RegioCitadis of Alstom (similar to the tram-train vehicles running in the region of Kassel, Germany). From Rotterdam, metro line E has been extended via a new tunnel and the converted railway line to The Hague Central Station – operated by high-floor LRVs RSG3 of the Bombardier Flexity Swift family. The *RandstadRail* light rail system has become a major transport success after many years of preparation and an unfortunate start (it opened in 2006 and almost immediately shut down for almost 1 year due to technical failures).

Initially TOD characteristics of the new light rail system were modest. This is not surprising because planning and even construction of the new neighbourhoods and centres in The Hague and Rotterdam were already in progress during the 1990s. At the same time *RandstadRail* remained a very insecure plan. The pace of progress was limited while new variants and budgets popped up

RandstadRail (Netherlands): Our Main Showcase Light Rail—cont'd

incrementally. Eventually it took over 15 years to reach the final decision in 2002 for the go-ahead of a compromise project, namely the construction of two overlapping systems operated, respectively, with tramway style light rail (from The Hague) and metro style light rail (from Rotterdam).

Moreover, TOD wasn't particularly favourited by some municipalities along the light rail system. They didn't consider their towns as part of a cohesive metropolitan area, hence, their urban programs along *RandstadRail* stations (for example, in Pijnacker-Nootdorp) were deliberately halted or delayed. The same applied for park and ride facilities. Nevertheless, *RandstadRail* is expected to structure urban development (densification, redevelopment, etc.) over the coming decades. Metropolitan growth seems unavoidable and meanwhile RandstadRail has been accepted by all parties. So, after about 10 years of operation, TOD really is practiced. In addition, the two main stations of The Hague and Rotterdam, which are connected by *RandstadRail*, have become spectacularly enhanced regional and national TOD nodes.

Station Lansingerland-Zoetermeer is the proposed hub and terminus for the extension of *RandstadRail* RR4 due to open in 2018. Design by Arcadis/Team V, commisioned by *Gemeente* Zoetermeer. *(Image courtesy: Arcadis.)*

Like Utrecht (also in the Netherlands) and Manchester in the UK, the metropolitan region of The Hague and Rotterdam could benefit from a tram-train. The feasibility of usage of this hybrid mode to boost the expansion of *RandstadRail* is not definite, although discussions have been started, for instance on a possible extension to Leiden; moreover various 'conventional' extensions are subject to debate (situation in 2017), while extension of RR4 is due to begin in 2018 and additional services on a section of the Rotterdam line E are seriously being considered.

Toyama (Japan) Showcase Light Rail

Author Rob van der Bijl (left) during fieldwork guided by Tetsuo Muro (centre), Councillor of the Urban Development Department of Toyama City Office.

The city of Toyama is home to our Japanese showcase light rail project and one of our TOD cases in Asia, and has been intensively explored during fieldwork. Japan was once the front runner with light rail developments. Particularly, the 1920s were memorable years, when numerous new light rail systems opened. In the post-war years many of these systems shrank, decayed or simply closed (e.g., Sendai, 1976; Gifu, 2005), although some were upgraded to full railways or to metros.

Our case of Toyama marks the final return of cutting-edge light rail to Japan. In April 2006, the first impulse to the implementation of Toyama's urban planning and mobility ambitions was due with the completion of the *Portram* project, the nation's paragon project for light rail. The ailing harbour railway, stretching over more than 8 km, has been refurbished into an urban tramway linking up to the back of the Japanese Railways main station by way of a new road section of more than 1 km. The *Portram* forms a good connection between the main station on the edge of the centre and the coastal area. By way of its new, carefully designed and interspersed stops, the tram is of much better service to travellers than the old train. The floor of the handsomely designed trams is low and thus facilitates 'threshold-free' changing from tram via platform to the public space. This public space has also received a great incentive along the whole tramway. Moreover, tram stops attract new building activity. On the side of the coast, the arrival of the tram immediately gave rise to new tourist facilities. The LRVs are of TLR0600

Toyama (Japan) Showcase Light Rail—cont'd

type, manufactured by Niigata Transys with Bombardier and are attractively designed.

Toyama aims to use TOD to fight urban sprawl. With the ageing and declining population, one cannot afford any further expansion. Instead urban development will have to be concentrated. *Portram* represents the first stage in this regard. It enhances the accessibility of urban facilities and supports densification. In this vision the Inner city and its amenities should be densified and improved too, including new facilities to boost tourism. That is why the strategic choice to improve the town's accessibility has been made — one of the most important prerequisites to sustainability and attractiveness. For this reason the existing tramway was improved and expanded in 2009 with a city loop tramway called 'Centram' (using the same type of LRVs as *Portam*). The line is operated anticlockwise and serves all the major centre sites, amenities and tourist hotspots. Since the arrival of the high-speed train, Shinkansen, in 2015, all three city tramways have had a shared stop under the new elevated train station. In the near future there will be a connection between *Portram* and the present tram network. This will create a direct link between the coast and the heart of the inner city.

Toyama's light rail system enhances the accessibility of urban facilities and supports densification.

In the more distant future, there are plans to regionalize the tram. One of the present regional railways will then be converted for operation by trams. The *Portram* will be able to ride on to the hinterland and the foot of the mountains via a new through connection with the city tramways. Then Toyama and its

Continued

Toyama (Japan) Showcase Light Rail—cont'd

region will have an integrated public transport network at its disposal, in which tram, bus and train enhance the inner city's optimal accessibility — thus contributing, according to plan, giving it a socioeconomic boost as well as countering unbridled urbanization. In this way, Toyama shows how light rail may aid in addressing the adverse effects on a city of an ageing and declining population.

Toyama serves as a pathfinder for future light rail in Japan. It has inspired numerous cities to improve their tramways. New light rail systems have been considered (e.g., in Tokyo) and in September 2016 the transport ministry approved plans for a new light rail system in Utsunomiya, the capital of Tochigi prefecture, north of Tokyo.

Kaohsiung (Taiwan): The First Light Rail

Impression of operation of the first preliminary stage in 2016. At this stop roof-mounted supercapacitors are charged via the vehicle's pantograph.

Kaohsiung, Taiwan, with the *Circular Line* project, is our Asian state-of-the-art light rail and TOD case. This project represents the first light rail system in Taiwan with at least two more to come (New Taipei City and Taichung). This case has underlined the importance of our Asian fieldworks.

In the early 1900s many tramways existed in Asia, particularly in South-east Asia, for instance in Bangkok (Thailand), Jakarta (Indonesia) and Singapore. With the exception of Japan, most of these tramways were abolished in the first half of the previous century. Taiwan is now one of the countries in Asia witnessing the return of light rail. The city of Kaohsiung, the second city in Taiwan with 1.5 million inhabitants, started with preparations in 2004 with a demonstration

Kaohsiung (Taiwan): The First Light Rail—cont'd

line in Central Park and continued with the actual project in 2012. The first preliminary stage opened in 2016 (after trials the previous year). The full first phase is due for operation in 2018.

The first stage is implemented along a former freight railway along the waterfront. The full circular system will offer connections with the two radial metro lines (both opened in 2008) at four stops. The tramway serves important attractions such as the large Dream Mall, Kaohsiung Exhibition Centre and the Main Public Library. Though the 2004 demonstration tramway was designed and constructed by Siemens, and operated with its Combino vehicle, the current tramway is operated with CAF LRVs, type Urbos 3, equipped with the CAF-developed 'Acumulador de Carga Rapida' (ACR) system. Roof-mounted super-capacitors are charged via the vehicle's pantograph at intermediate stops with no overhead line in between. In addition, similar LRVs are delivered by CAF for systems such as those in Bilbao (Spain), Birmingham (UK), Cincinnati (Ohio, US), Luxembourg, Pittsburgh (Pennsylvania, US), Zaragoza (Spain) and finally our *Uithof line* case in Utrecht (Netherlands).

The full circle will be constructed in the upcoming second stage of the project. At that time the waterfront section of the ultimately planned circular system will prove its transport value and impressive potential for TOD.

LRVs just arrived from Spain and being prepared for the first trials in 2015.

Meanwhile light rail is due to expand in other places in Taiwan too. Since 2014 a light rail system has been under construction in New Taipei City (opening planned for 2018). A system in the city of Taichung is in the planning stage, moreover Taiwan's government announced in 2017 a project that entails a tram-train between Taipei and Keelung City.

CHAPTER 4

Argumentation in Favour of Light Rail

Investments in public facilities can be justified based on several grounds. This also goes for high-quality public transport, which is an obvious facility, and a light rail project is an example of this. It is an urban facility and has far-stretching spatial consequences because of the infrastructural components. The definition of light rail in Chapter 2 shows that being rail-bound distinguishes light rail from urban bus projects. Financing, fitting it into the urban landscape, and maintenance are taken into consideration when infrastructural decisions have to be made.

It turns out that there are five essential domains in the argumentation for light rail. They have been successively branded as *effective mobility*, *efficient city*, *economy*, *environment*, and *equity* and are also known as the five E's.

When it comes to light rail *effective mobility* mainly concerns effective operation. *Efficient city* is about the extent to which light rail qualities can be achieved using urban design/planning and traffic design/planning. Direct and indirect effects of light rail, like change in the value of land and property, are placed under *economy*. *Environment* is about all the aspects of light rail that contribute to a sustainable environment. *Equity* is all about how light rail promotes social equality and is of specific importance in light rail projects in France, England and the US.

Our cases on tram projects in cities like Paris, Strasbourg, Los Angeles and Detroit make it clear that light rail argumentation consists of multiple components, including the civic and public domains like social coherence and the prevention of social exclusion. The five domains of argumentation (Fig. 4.1) can be summarized as follows:

Effective mobility (E1) — effectiveness of transport and mobility.

Efficient city (E2) — suitability of spatial use and spatial/urban (re) development.

Economy (E3) — prosperity and wellbeing in/for cities.

Environment (E4) — decreasing carbon footprints; sustainable cities.

Equity (E5) — socially inclusive cities.

Light Rail Transit Systems
ISBN 978-0-12-814784-9
https://doi.org/10.1016/B978-0-12-814784-9.00004-9

The latter three E's tend to be grouped together and are also known as the three P's: *Profit* (Economy), *Planet* (Environment), and *People* (Equity).

Figure 4.1 Five essential domains of argumentation. *(Graph designed by Rob van der Bijl and Niels van Oort.)*

4.1 EFFECTIVE MOBILITY

Deciding whether or not light rail is an effective or at least suitable mode for a certain public transport task is often subject to ideological debate. Discussions about function and necessity of a tramway are held by supporters of certain views, or by 'believers' in tram, bus or whichever form of public transport and mode. A well-supported decision has to be based on the neutral value of the effectiveness of the proposed mode, like light rail or bus. The value should be self-evident, and so without any preference for light rail or any other form of public transport. Different studies into common modes of transport, like tram and bus, show that suitability and, therefore, effectiveness are intertwined with the scale and scope of the specific demand for transport within an urban environment. Fairly recent work by Carmen Hass-Klau et al. is a good example of this. Several studies by these researchers have provided insight into the considerations about the choice between, for example, light rail and high-quality bus. We expand on the value of effectiveness of transport characteristics in our *RandstadRail* case later in this book. The general graph by Goudappel Coffeng can be used to explain different levels of transport.

Light rail corresponds with the first three levels, which are local, metropolitan and conurbation, but with emphasis on the urban–regional level. It is plausible that this outcome is relevant for most European countries that have cities similar in size and density. On the other hand, in the US, where cities tend to have lower densities, lower ridership is accepted to plan and justify light rail and tramway/streetcar projects. Asia is the opposite — higher ridership values are required there. Recent tram projects in China show relatively high figures. The transition from bus to tram is not cost-effective in less-developed countries.

The graph by Goudappel Coffeng (Fig. 4.2) shows substantial overlap between different bandwidths. This implies that the final choice for a certain mode of transport depends greatly on context: local conditions help make the final decision, for instance bus instead of tram. Some of these conditions can still lead to opting for the mode of bus, in spite of relatively high ridership (for instance, when there is no on-site tram infrastructure at all). The opposite is possible, too, when in spite of low figures a tram is required (for example, when a historic city centre with narrow streets is not suitable for bus operation). In other cases the choice for tram, bus or a different mode strongly depends on local culture and industrial conditions (like a tram factory or car tire manufacturer in the area), or special events (like a fair).

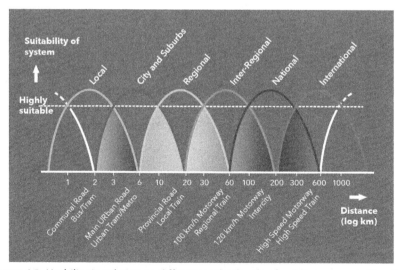

Figure 4.2 Usability in relation to different scales/levels of public transport. *(Graph by Goudappel-Coffeng (Niels van Oort).)*

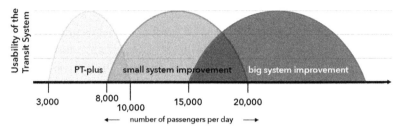

Figure 4.3 Usability in relation to different bandwidths of transport value and according to different modes of public transport. *(Graph by Goudappel-Coffeng (Niels van Oort).)*

In Western Europe the required bandwidth for effective light rail operation is about 20,000 passengers per direction per day. This is three to four times higher than for a conventional bus and about twice more than is required for a double-articulated bus. The finally required ridership numbers are highly dependent on context. In spite of this, Goudappel Coffeng offers a graph that includes three bandwidths for ridership values, which shows numbers relevant for specific types of public transport (Fig. 4.3).

When the bandwidth of 20,000 passengers per day is reached light rail is the first mode that should be considered, even before bus, metro or regional rail. Sometimes the choice for light rail is obvious. Our *Uithof line* case in Utrecht is an example of this. Operational costs and required reliability simply cannot be achieved effectively by using any other mode than tram. Even an advanced bus technology like the double-articulated bus has been shown to remain an inadequate solution.

Ridership alone turns out to be sufficient to justify light rail in our collection of cases. Some projects, including our Groningen (Netherlands) case of *RegioTram*, were assessed by critics based on presumed low ridership. Effective transport is a valid argument for investments in projects and plans, but in most cases other types of arguments were used for the justification of light rail. These four other types of argumentation will be discussed in the following sections.

The Rail–Bicycle System

The effectiveness of light rail can be further enhanced if the way travelers get to the stops is optimized. Cars have a role here, but this is only suitable for a limited number of transfer nodes where cars can get relatively quickly, without causing too much inconvenience in the area. Walking is, of course, also important; every public transport traveller is pedestrian at the start and at end of his or her journey. And then there's the bicycle. In many cities worldwide cycling in combination with public transport has risen dramatically in recent years.

The Rail–Bicycle System—cont'd

A 'rail–bike system' has been developed in several places, and has just begun to work as a new modality.

Our analyses of Dutch light rail projects show that cycling is often seen as a rival to public transport (and vice versa). But, in fact, both modes of transport are complementary. Shorter distances (2–5 km) in Dutch cities are often bridged by bicycle, whereas in French cities, most people travel these distances by tram. However, on longer urban–regional distances, bikes (and e-bikes) can be seen as complementary in order to bridge the 'first and last mile'. In this regard investments in light rail stations and stops are necessary.

Example of Dutch state of the art cycle parking. One of the two new facilities near Amsterdam South Station and World Trade Centre. The shown parking *'Fietsgarage Mahlerplein'* (opened November 2016; 3000 places; designed by Paul van der Ree, StudioK/Movares) contributes efficiently to the performance of the rail–bicycle system.

Continued

The Rail—Bicycle System—cont'd

Often, parking of bicycles at stations and stops is considered as a problem with multiple characteristics — insufficient capacity, high management costs, inaccessible public space, etc. Without ignoring these problems, it has to be said that this is also a sign of success. As much as 40% of train passengers in the Netherlands use the bicycle (situation in 2013). This is an effective form of 'chain mobility', made possible by the fact that the Netherlands has both a good bicycle and a good train infrastructure. Unfortunately, there are no figures for the bicycle—train chain on regional distances, or of a similar chain in which light rail performs a function.

Unfortunately, the chain at the arrival side is less strong, because travelers are less likely to ride a bike there. A solution would be to take the bike by train, metro or tram, but there are many objections, especially the limited capacity of trains and LRVs, and moreover obstacles on entry and exit. Therefore, it is better to use another bicycle at the destination. This means that much capacity is needed at the arrival station. The success of the Dutch public bicycle-sharing system 'OV fiets' (Public Transport Bicycle, the largest system of its kind in the world) is a result of the bicycle availability at destination stations. To continue this success, availability must be guaranteed.

Bicycle use and ownership in the Netherlands is high. This is both a condition and cause of successful chain mobility. It is questionable whether a more flexible public bicycle sharing system, such as the Vélib' formula in France, would make the chain even stronger. The strong point of the Dutch rail—bicycle system is the ability to cycle from an origin to various stations or stops. More than half of the Dutch live less than 5 km from a train station, and a quarter of the population even less than 1.5 km. These are favourable figures, made more favourable by the many light rail stops in Dutch cities.

4.2 EFFICIENT CITY

Urban designers and traffic engineers should take into consideration light rail and similar high-quality public transport that requires integrated infrastructure. When incorporated into the designing and planning phases, light rail qualities can be utilized to their fullest extents, resulting in feasible and useful projects. It is therefore regrettable that urban design is reduced to catering to aesthetic requirements, and limited to improving the city image and atmosphere. Aesthetics and atmosphere are important qualities; nonetheless, reducing their role in urban design and planning would do right by light rail. Aesthetics and atmosphere are factors that have played important parts in several light rail projects, resulting in iconic effects and branding opportunities for cities. However, the function and efficiency of urban design/planning and traffic design/ planning are more comprehensive, because they include several functions.

Firstly, light rail can play a decisive part in designing public space. Over the past years many examples have been gathered in best practice guides, like the Interreg project HiTrans, in which principles and strategies were developed to create high-quality public transport in cities and urban regions. In spite of this, the introduction of light rail is often seen as a violation of the quality and use of public space, which is, in fact, the case when it has not been designed properly. Prejudice resulting from bad design can cause negative opinions. This much is true: many examples show a challenging potential to use light rail to strengthen urban functions and qualities. The same goes for related traffic design that allows the division of urban space into zones and improves safety, circulation and accessibility.

Secondly, light rail is an efficient tool for urban and regional planning. Examples of this have been assembled for projects like the previously mentioned HiTrans. Light rail turns out to be able to restructure the city and urban region. The same goes for neighbourhoods, quarters and precincts, including areas that are on the decline. Light rail as urban– regional public transport is a powerful tool to oppose unrestrained urban growth.

Thirdly, light rail can be considered a major condition for urban development and planning. Light rail and similar forms of public transport on imbedded and fixed infrastructure (like metro) can improve urban connection and local accessibility. Their fixed infrastructure guarantees a technical and economic life span of at least 30 years, while 60 years or more is possible. This means that the connections and local accessibilities brought about by this infrastructure can be useful for a very long time. More remote areas further away and difficult to reach can be connected and accessed when the infrastructure is extended. This helps create new, favourable conditions for further (re)development of these areas.

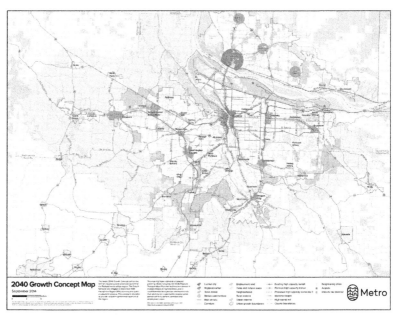

Metro's '2040 Growth Concept Map' — the 'TOD plan' of Portland, Oregon (US): light rail as carrier of urban (re)development. *(Map by Metro, September 2014.)*

The fourth function of light rail has already been mentioned in earlier chapters. Light rail as a form of 'transit', an American term to denote high-quality urban public transport, can contribute significantly to the realization of transit oriented development (TOD). The fixed infrastructure that comes with light rail can provide structure, which is useful for TOD because it helps centre real estate and property investments around stations and stops, in particular stops that function as transfer hubs. Multiple studies in America, Europe, and, more recently, Asia have proved the value of TOD. TOD has also been applied in China. It turns out from our cases in Japan (Toyama) and Taiwan (Kaohsiung) that the combination of TOD and light rail offers promising integration of space and mobility. In the Netherlands, research supervised by professor Luca Bertolini was conducted at the university of Amsterdam. TOD turns out to be a particularly successful tool when light rail services important urban centres by providing several stops that open up entire station environments, as well as the surrounding area and surrounding urban region. Investing in economic activities like destination areas is profitable in the light of TOD. Concentrating employment and activities around public facilities increases the effect of light rail. It actually strengthens the characteristics that were mentioned earlier in this chapter.

However, successful implementation is more easily said than done. Wendy Tan (from Bertolini's research group) brought forth a number of limiting conditions in her PhD thesis. Particular attention is paid to what she calls 'formal barriers', like institutional complexity and fragmentation. These lead to a clear division of roles and a clear final responsibility. Tan also recognizes informal barriers, like lack of urgency and indifference towards public transport. The latter implies that the value of light rail is not actually recognized, let alone accepted. We will return to this matter in Chapter 7 on our case of the Groningen tram project.

4.3 ECONOMY

There are light rail initiators who expect economic development and growth as soon as their system is operational. They consider this kind of economic effects of light rail as a sort of holy grail of urban development and increased values for land and real estate. However, just like other forms of high-quality public transport, light rail does not operate autonomously or automatically. This does not mean, though, that light rail cannot aid in prompting or recovering economic growth. Unfortunately, there are no direct, let alone causative, economic effects shown from light rail.

In spite of this, well-served light rail stops and stations represent favourable conditions for economic development, which can stimulate investments when combined with other factors. Improved accessibility of locations is particularly meaningful for this development and, therefore, the value of (future) urban development. In some cases light rail can have an iconic effect, for instance, around some well-designed stops in gentrified areas like the Pearl District in Portland, Oregon, or in attractive and historic city centres in Europe, like the renovated centre of Strasbourg. There is no doubt that the symbolic and iconic meanings of *The Streetcar* or *Le Tramway* stimulated private and public investments. A vast amount of research is available, for example, the previously mentioned Carmen Hass-Klau, which shows that light rail is an important condition for urban development with positive economic effects. Researchers like Hass-Klau emphasize that these effects only showed in combination with relevant interventions, initiatives, investments, and other forms of support. Not only do private parties with interest in profit play an important part in that, but also public parties, in particular the (local) government that stimulates, co-ordinates and facilitates infrastructure and economic development.

In the absence of light rail and necessary high-quality accessibility it is automatically more difficult to secure and stimulate investments and other initiatives. In addition, the effectiveness of urban development policy decreases in the absence of good public transport. In their elaborate study on the economic effects of investments in light rail, Richard Knowles and Fiona Ferbrache assessed the absence of what they call 'a well-developed and modern transport system', even as a severe limitation of economic growth. On the other hand, they also found that the value of land and real estate generally increases and that it is possible for developers to contribute to investments in the area when its accessibility has been improved by light rail. Improved connection and accessibility of the area offer other parties involved, like entrepreneurs and public organizations, the opportunity to contribute to economic activity. Correlated to this, Knowles and Ferbrache mention 'inward investments' caused by increased light rail activity. They do note that it is very difficult to pinpoint which investments can be solely attributed to light rail.

Just because inward investments attributed to light rail cannot unambiguously be recognized or measured this does not mean they do not exist. On the contrary, these investments in centres of medium-sized and large cities are very obvious when it comes to shops and cultural and recreational facilities. To some extent such investments play a role in renovating and developing urban regional centres. Carmen Hass-Klau et al. have studied retail transformation caused by the arrival of the tram in Strasbourg city centre. They concluded that smaller shops were replaced by premium-segment retail chains. This transformation is confirmed in a study by the former CERTU ('Le Centre d'études sur les réseaux, les transports, l'urbanisme et les constructions publiques'), both for our Strasbourg case and other new 'tram cities' in France. CERTU researchers emphasize the change in quality; shops of lesser quality have been replaced with luxury facilities. A simultaneous consequence was an increase in rents and real estate value, resulting in smaller shopkeepers no longer being able to afford their premises in city centres. This phenomenon can be summarized as gentrification of shopping facilities in city centres. Large retailers and their inward investments upscale shopping facilities, which draws considerably more shoppers to centres of tram cities like Strasbourg.

We can conclude from our analyses of Dutch light rail projects that inward investments in city centres are also relevant. In the course of the 1990s the effects on retail were noticeable, as can be concluded from work for the *Souterrain* project (part of our *RandstadRail* project case) in The

Hague. Many shops of lesser quality closed, but in all fairness it should be noted that this coincided with years of renovation works. The *Souterrain* ('basement' in Dutch) is a tunnel that combines two tram stations and an underground car park. Two urban tramway lines and the *RandstadRail* lines to Zoetermeer run through the tunnel. The arrival of *Souterrain* and *RandstadRail*, together with adjustments to car traffic, have greatly improved the accessibility of The Hague city centre. While conditions in The Hague have been improved by inward investments, cancelling the Groningen *RegioTram* (our other main case) was a missed opportunity. Poor inner-city streets would benefit especially from such investments.

A side remark needs to be added to the light rail successes in cities like Strasbourg and The Hague. The scope of economic investments and the increased turnover are never or hardly ever weighed up against the building costs and operation costs of the tram system. Several studies, including the one by Knowles and Ferbrache, confirm this. Thanks to light rail, the accessibility of town centres improves, the value of land and real estate increases, and entrepreneurs make a profit, but this does not mean the private sector contributes to construction and operation costs. It is possible to encourage or even make the private sector contribute, but still the newly created value is rarely shared with government bodies. This challenge is called *value capture* in literature. It does not happen in our Dutch case cities, though there are (future) possibilities to this end. A group of researchers from Radboud University Nijmegen led by Erwin van der Krabben, professor of planning and property development, has extensively researched value capturing. They also listed several financial instruments.

4.4 ENVIRONMENT

It is remarkable that environmental factors tend to be omitted in (applied) light rail research. Part of this has to do with the fact that environmental effects of public transport in general are difficult to determine, especially when quantitative values are desired.

In spite of this, some characteristics of light rail provide certainty in this respect; electric traction causes less air pollution in the immediate proximity of a tramway, as well as less noise pollution and vibration compared to a situation with non-electric modes.

Environmental factors are generally not or hardly taken into consideration when assessing light rail projects. These factors play a very modest part in the debate about future public transport. Several European countries, for instance the UK and the Netherlands, have not included these values quantitatively in their cost—benefit analyses, in spite of light rail providing favourable conditions for the immediate surroundings, the city, and the entire metropolitan region. These shortcomings in the decision support method will be covered more elaborately in our Utrecht *Uithof line* case in Chapter 6.

What has been determined is that light rail contributes substantially to an improvement in the local environment that was previously serviced by traditional buses. Air pollution decreases because fewer particulates are emitted and noise pollution decreases likewise. Less vehicle movement is needed because of the relatively high transport capacity of light rail, especially when opting for car-free zones. This is a great improvement for the urban environment, especially when traffic flow is reduced in large parts of the city.

Four principles have been summarized in order to understand the full extent of the environmental benefits of light rail (compiled and presented for the first time by the author Rob van der Bijl at a conference about sustainable development of the European Business Council in Tokyo, April 2012).

Inspired by the 'green traffic hierarchy', as was applied by the New York interest group for cycling, walking and environmentally friendly traffic, the four principles have been placed in chronological order: (1) less transport; (2) collective transport; (3) fixed infrastructure; and (4) sustainable technologies.

These principles are discussed and illustrated in the next section.

Four Principles of Sustainability

The environmental advantages of light rail have been sorted into four principles. The chronology is important; the first principle should be listed first, followed by the second, third and fourth principle respectively.

First Principle: Less Transport

In the interest of the environment the urban carbon footprint should be as small as possible. This means that the size of a city should be minimalized, while the density should be maximized. Light rail benefits small urban sizes, because it requires relatively high transport demand and works well in high urban densities. Complementary measures like urban planning and policy can increase and continue effective use of light rail.

The metropolitan regions of Atlanta (Georgia, US) and Barcelona (Spain) serve as examples of such a relevant comparison. Their respective surface areas are 4280 and 3235 km², while both metropolises have the same number of inhabitants (about 5 million). Mobility-induced CO_2 emissions are lower in *Regió*

Four Principles of Sustainability—cont'd

Metropolitana de Barcelona (RMB) than they are in Atlanta. This comparison is somewhat too optimistic, because the Barcelona city centre (101 km^2 and 1.62 million inhabitants) was constructed more densely and is used more intensively than the similar area around downtown Atlanta. Besides, Barcelona and its immediate surroundings (*Àrea Metropolitana de Barcelona* — 636 km^2 and 3.24 million inhabitants) have extensive metro and light rail systems, while the metropolitan area is catered by (regional) railways. The Atlanta metro system is limited in size (two lines) and there is only one small city tramway (since December 2014). A network of regional rail lines has been considered for years, while construction has not yet started.

Second Principle: Collective Transport

A modal shift from individual to collective transport is the foundation of sustainable mobility. Public transport as the main form of collective transport is effective for all sustainable subjects, such as reduction in energy usage and greenhouse gas emissions. The well-known three photographs on the Strasbourg tram project illustrate this: the same street with the same number of passengers is shown, transported in a large number of cars, three buses, and finally one tram, respectively. The message is clear. Even if the three buses were conventional ones running on diesel, the collective passengers' footprints would still be smaller than the motorists', even if they drove electric or hybrid cars. The environmental achievement of trams is evident. Light rail is a pragmatic and suitable form of public transport and contributes to sustainable operation of collective transport in cities and urban regions. Our Strasbourg case is a striking example of this because it has become an iconic system.

Third Principle: Fixed Infrastructure

Tram in Barcelona: on fixed-rail infrastructure.

Continued

Four Principles of Sustainability—cont'd

Cities can be reduced in size, but increased in density, by aiming urban growth and redevelopment at existing transport corridors (see the first principle). Public transport as the major form of collective transport (see the second principle) will be able to be operated more efficiently, because many users stay, live, and work close to public transport. The advantages that are connected to the first two principles can be amplified by fixing the infrastructure as, for instance, rail-based public transport. By making a conscious decision against flexible modes (like traditional buses) and in favour of fixed, rail-bound forms of public transport, a sustainable condition for (re)development emerges that will be aimed more and more at collective mobility. In other words: public transport based on fixed infrastructure structures cities and urban regions in a sustainable way.

Light rail is an excellent example of this kind of public transport. Light rail provides fixed-infrastructure connections in and with cities and efficiently opens up the urban surroundings. Light rail becomes even more efficient when existing infrastructure is used. From a sustainable point of view it does not necessarily make sense to construct new light rail lines. Making more efficient use of existing infrastructure should be prioritized; constructing new infrastructure should only be considered if there is no other option. But even then it can be efficient to reuse (routes of) old infrastructure. The first phase of tramway *T2* in Paris is a good example of this, as well as our case on tramway *T4* (2006) in the Parisian suburbs. This line was created by reconstructing the old Bondy to Aulnay-sous-Bois (*Ligne des Coquetiers*) railway to accommodate a tram operation. Another example is the project of the *Exposition Line* in our case city of Los Angeles. Here, the route of the former *Pacific Electric Santa Monica Air Line* is used for a new light rail from the city centre to the coast. In Birmingham, UK, (not one of our cases) the route of an old railway was used when the first stage of a new tramway was settled upon.

Fourth Principle: Sustainable Technologies

Sustainable mobility in the form of light rail can be strengthened by complementing it with other sustainable modes, like train and metro. The next step is complementing public transport with other forms of sustainable mobility, first and foremost walking and cycling. It is beyond any doubt that these are connected to public transport. Nearly all travellers begin and end their trips as pedestrians. The implementation of sustainable technologies can optimize the system of walking and travelling by public transport, using information technology, for instance. The same goes for cycling, but cycling has greater potential to increase the range of public transport than walking has. The range of an origin stop (the stop where a trips begins) of a light rail system becomes larger by providing facilities for cyclists, like parking places and maintenance. Cycling

Four Principles of Sustainability—cont'd

can also increase the range of the destination stops (where a trip ends). *Vélib'* in Paris and the *OV-Fiets* (public transport bike) in Dutch cities are examples of this.

Optimal implementation of sustainable technologies is the last part of this fourth principle. It is not possible to overly cover these technologies here, but it is not difficult to imagine a sustainable and logistic system to complement a public transport system in cities and urban areas. The Zürich cargo tram proves an unusual example of sustainable logistics. The tram infrastructure is used to collect rubbish and take it to a collection station on the west side of the city. The rubbish is collected there and taken to recycling factories by lorries. The use of the electricity infrastructure (overhead lines, ground-level power supply) of trams or trolley buses for other forms of urban mobility is a field yet to be explored. This would aid the aim of electrically powering as much mobility as possible in city centres. Sustainable technologies do not have to concern only the physical infrastructure; personal trip planners can drastically improve public transport and several multimodal trip planners are already available. Another example is the availability of lessons to teach drivers of trams or trains to drive more economically; or changing to LED lighting helps save energy at stations and stops.

4.5 EQUITY

Like environmental factors, (applied) light rail research often lacks topics to do with equity, or they play only a marginal role. Topics like social segregation and civic cohesion tend to play a minor role in considering light rail and other high-quality public transport. This has to do with the fact that it is very difficult to analyse and assess the social effects of light rail, let alone quantify them. Traditional societal cost–benefit analyses underestimate or simply do not include these effects. The former mainly applies to the Dutch practice, because in countries like France, the UK and the US attention is given to equity when light rail projects are justified, planned and constructed. However, in Asia and the rest of the world so far this issue hasn't been explored (with exception of Australia and New Zealand).

New tramways in France, the UK and the US are generally considered to contribute to recovering social cohesion and making it sustainable. Light rail plays an important part in promoting inclusion (prevention of social exclusion). Similarly, the usual social considerations, like access to employment, shops and public facilities, also need to be considered. Access to social networks and relatives is also mentioned.

Access to employment is seen as a basic necessity for social inclusion. It makes sense to assign light rail a part in this, because facilitating commuting has always been the main task of public transport. We researched the notorious riots in the Los Angeles neighbourhood of Watts as part of our case study into the history of LA light rail. So far this seems to confirm the importance of good public transport when it comes to providing social access to work. The last ride of the *Red Car* of the notable *Pacific Electric* was in 1961, only 4 years prior to the riots. The Watts residents had no real alternative to accessing employment in central Los Angeles and the harbour of Long Beach when the rail connection disappeared. The social situation and unemployment in particular were important causes of the Watts riots. The absence of adequate public transport for commuting was one of the (many) reasons for social exclusion and unrest.

Difficult access to work as a consequence of absent public transport connections is most pressing in urban areas where car ownership is low. Especially underprivileged parts of cities risk social exclusion as a result of inadequate public transport. Our Detroit case study shows that the parts of central Detroit with insufficient public transport are also faced with low car ownership. This combination of 'no public transport' and 'no car' shows the lack of privilege and is at the same time a huge potential for public transport that is needed to provide connections with employment or chances of work in different parts of town. This is why Woodward Avenue, a central corridor of poverty, was selected as the main axis for a new tram connection. The Detroit tramway was shut down in 1956 and 60 years later it returned as the *Woodward Avenue Streetcar* when this tramway opened in May 2017. This project, also known as the *M-1 Rail Line*, symbolizes the social part light rail can play in a city.

Strengthening social cohesion and fighting social–spatial segregation was an important goal of the new generation of tram projects in France. Unfortunately, the function of the tram in this respect was not evident. Achieving (renewed) social cohesion in cities is not an easy task. The arrival of the tram has certainly had social effects, but it has not lead to any evident change in the urban outlook on social segregation. It turns out to be very difficult to make the *banlieues* (suburbs) part of the city.

The previously mentioned research institute CERTU has used its analyses of French cities after the arrival of trams to confirm that this new form of public transport has to perform within a dynamic situation, not a static one. It was established in our case city of Strasbourg that the new tramway worked as an accelerator and amplifier of existing social tendencies in a dynamic context. The matter of equity had not been specified here, but the analysis by CERTU is reason to believe that the arrival of the tram amplified the existing tendency to further social-spatial segregation, instead of the reversed effect. This presumption was confirmed, though not officially, in an interview with an urban designer of the municipality of Strasbourg some years ago. Facilities in the city centre have turned out to be more luxurious since the introduction of the tram, which confirms Carmen Hass-Klau's research results. The city centre has become fancy, maybe too fancy. This gentrification may have caused residents of the suburbs to avoid the city centre, possibly because the shops have become too expensive for them. In any case, it is plausible that the central public space has become alien territory for residents of the suburbs. Here, the tram has amplified segregation.

However, it is beyond any doubt that trams supply a necessary public facility in cities like Strasbourg. From the start the tramway has served as a good connection between the residential areas in the suburbs and employment in the city centre. In addition, in the suburbs the tramway is frequently used for travelling from home to local facilities, thus serving local social cohesion.

The social function of public transport is seen as a safety net or backup plan in many countries. Public transport is a last resort for people who have no means of transport of their own at their disposal. When a stop is proposed to be eliminated, for instance to straighten a bus line, opponents always claim the public transport function of a social safety net. We conclude from our analyses on Dutch light rail projects that this has not helped successful implementation of these projects. Unlike in France, trams are not seen as the bringers of social cohesion; quite the contrary, actually. The arrival of a tramway almost always entails revision of the existing network, so stops disappear or distances to stops increase somewhat. This turns out to be a reason to keep criticizing tram projects heavily. Compared to the American situation it is striking how in the Netherlands and many other European countries car ownership (or the possibility to use one) is seen as a given. Apparently no thought is given to the fact that reduced prosperity or downright poverty can lead to a different situation, similar to the American one. This could be a reason to look at the social effects of light rail in a different light.

On Transformations From Heavy Rail to Light Rail

Transformations of heavy rail services into more effective and efficient light rail services on existing railways feature some basic characteristics of tramway style operation of railways. We share four of our cases in this regard. These cases convinced us that transformations from heavy to light rail under some conditions contribute to effective mobility, efficient use of urban areas and also to enhancement of economy, environment and equity. Our four cases in summary:

- Zwolle—Kampen (Netherlands):
  Conversion to tramway study.
- Paris, Aulnay-sous-Bois—Bondy (France), *T4*:
  Conversion to tramway project.
- Gouda-Alphen (Netherlands), *RijnGouwelijn*:
  Operation of light rail pilot.
- Lyon/Saint-Paul—Sain-Bel (France), *Tram-train de l'ouest Lyonnais*:
  Operation of light rail project.

Zwolle—Kampen (Netherlands)

Cover of our study: 'Conversion to tramway as pacer for renewing national railway provider ProRail'.

On Transformations From Heavy Rail to Light Rail—cont'd

This case is addressed in our prize-winning conversion-to-tramway study (2006–10). Implementation has been seriously considered, though finally replaced by an improved heavy rail project (2018).

Conversion to tramway has been thoroughly investigated in a study for the local railway between the Dutch towns of Zwolle and Kampen. Instead of one new classic train station halfway along the railway line, we proposed and designed in our study a series of tram stops in order to optimize planned urban (re)development (e.g., the precinct Stadshagen). These stops were envisaged as fully integrated in the public realm and would have offered excellent local accessibility with links to networks for pedestrians, bicycles and cars.

Two well-integrated tram stops optimize planned urban development (e.g., the precinct Stadshagen).

The Zwolle–Kampen case represents clearly our first model that entails a full conversion from railway to tramway. This radical approach doesn't exclude

Continued

On Transformations From Heavy Rail to Light Rail—cont'd

compromises and hybrid solutions but, first and foremost, what action needs to be taken to enable such a rigorous conversion from heavy to light rail has to be investigated. Our case study is still up to date. Not because the conversion to tramway was realized, unfortunately the tender for light rail operation has failed twice, but because of the exemplary effect. For future use the full-conversion concept is elaborated as a toolbox to enhance effective mobility and efficient land use.

We expect that in the long run this approach favours economy, environment and equity. After all, depending on context (time, local situation and constraints), different elements can be applied: operation models (e.g., mix with freight transport), legal aspects, rail technology and engineering, urban planning and design issues, environmental issues, institutional and organizational factors and, finally, economic and societal feasibility.

Paris, Aulnay-sous-Bois—Bondy (France), *T4*

Converted intersection near Gargan stop. Tram-train regulated with regular traffic signals.

This case entails conversion from heavy rail to light rail in the metropolitan area of Paris. This is the first fully French tram-train project (2006).

A very inspiring example of a conversion to a tramway project is 'T4' in the metropolitan area of Paris. This project entailed the full transformation of the

On Transformations From Heavy Rail to Light Rail—cont'd

8-km railway between Aulnay-sous-Bois and Bondy, historically known as 'Ligne des Coquetiers'. The new tramway service with Siemens Avanto LRVs was inaugurated in November 2006. Operated by the French national railways (SNCF) this former railway became the first so-called tram-train line in France. Under construction (in 2015) is a tramway style branch line to Montfermeil, a 'banlieue' in the east.

This second example of a full conversion to tramway has been elaborated for all relevant subjects. In terms of effective urban mobility and efficient urban planning, but also in terms of improved and attractive new models of public transport, conversion according to Greater Paris' T4 conversion to tramway is promising and also offers a real perspective on similar projects in Europe and elsewhere. In this regards various 'details' of the project are inspiring. For instance, some stops on T4 are new, while all other stops are reconstructed and adapted former stations. All these stops are pragmatically and efficiently integrated into their environment and provide appealing and clear information. All stops have low platforms. The frequency has been increased. Several years after opening, a parallel cycle path has been laid over almost the entire length of the tramway.

One note: despite the clear approach to favour tramway-style transport, the railway history is still present, for example, the power supply is still of a heavy rail type (25 kV AC); although the second line to Montfermeil is provided with 750 V DC.

Gouda-Alphen (Netherlands), *RijnGouwelijn*

A coupled set of LRVs (Bombardier, type A32) called at added low central platforms.

Continued

On Transformations From Heavy Rail to Light Rail—cont'd

This Dutch showcase light rail project is compared with projects that applied integrated contracts. The *RijnGouwelijn* is staged as a victim of laborious planning and incoherent political decision making that eventually killed the project. What we like to address here is the third part of this case: the tram-train pilot operation of light rail within a heavy rail environment on a section of the envisaged system (2003–9).

The third case, operation of a light rail pilot, represents a second model of conversion. Instead of full conversion to a tramway (as the previous two cases have shown) this second model implies the replacement of heavy rail vehicles (i.e., regular trains) by LRVs, in combination with modest adaptation of the railway infrastructure. Another example of a railway pragmatically adapted for tram operation is located in Île de France at the fringe of the Paris metropolis on the 10-km-long railway line between Esbly and Crécy-la-Chapelle, where since 2011 conventional trains have been replaced by Siemens Avanto LRVs (also used on T4; see previous case).

The experiences with the Dutch pilot were promising. All technical issues of operating LRVs (type A32 from Bombardier; also known from use in Stockholm, Sweden) like modes of detection, operational models and various security issues have been successfully addressed. Unfortunately, the results of the pilot couldn't be used in the *RijnGouwelijn* itself, since this project was cancelled in 2012. Meanwhile in France the Esbly–Crécy-la-Chapelle conversion, though very pragmatically organized, proved to be highly successful. Just a conversion to LRV operation boosted use in 1 year after the conversion by 17.6%. Station Couilly–Saint-Germain–Quincy showed a rise of 63.3%. Therefore we are confident conversion has a promising future, favouring effective mobility, efficient use of urban areas and also enhancement of economy, environment and equity.

On Transformations From Heavy Rail to Light Rail—cont'd

Map of proposed first and second phase of the *RijnGouwelijn*; including the route of the pilot Gouda-Alphen. *(Map by Smidswater.)*

Note:

The pilot would have support the *RijnGouwelijn* project: a showcase tram-train project in the Netherlands that entailed regional through running on

Continued

On Transformations From Heavy Rail to Light Rail—cont'd

heavy rail mainlines and new urban tramways serving the historic city of Leiden and two coastal towns. The plan contained all the ingredients of a successful implementation of TOD tailored by the province (project owner) and municipalities along the line. There were also financial agreements on land, property and real estate with key stakeholders such as Leiden University. However, in terms of political and administrative decision-making and societal support, planning proved to be extremely difficult. For years the project's progress was very unsure and its management ambiguous. In May 2012, deputies of the province finally pulled the plug and terminated this ambitious and challenging project. Eventually, in December 2016, the operation on the route of the former pilot (Gouda-Alphen) was contracted separately for train operations by Abellio and labelled as part of 'R-Net' of Randstad in the western Netherlands.

Lyon/Saint-Paul—Sain-Bel (France), *Tram-train de l'ouest Lyonnais*

A Citadis Dualis tram-train vehicle called at a low platform.

This case represents a light rail scheme for improving service on the regional railway from Lyon Saint-Paul station to Sain-Bel. This is one of our cases of a light rail operation within a heavy rail environment.

Since September 2012 the railway from Saint-Paul station in Lyon to Sain-Bel town has been operated by LRVs (type Citadis Dualis manufactured by Alstom). Hence, tram-train LRVs (using a new overhead) replaced classic diesel-electric trains, though still operating in a heavy rail technical and legal

On Transformations From Heavy Rail to Light Rail—cont'd

environment. Similar projects have been implemented elsewhere in France (e.g., Nantes region and Greater Paris).

Station L'Arbresle deserves special attention since it proves how heavy rail stations can be transformed into tramway-style stops without changing the heavy railway infrastructure. The public realm and platforms are smoothly integrated.

Station L'Arbresle disguised as a tram-like stop with easy ways of transferring to other modes of transport.

Boosting patronage on these old mainly rural railways has been the principal reason for the conversion from train to tram operations. So far the new service has been considered to be an improvement. Moreover, the new situation at station L'Arbresle looks promising with regard to achieving improved quality of the public realm and transfer facilities. The future will tell whether rural-like conditions along the whole line will also allow for significant economic, environmental and social improvements.

CHAPTER 5

Augmented Quality Due to Light Rail

Light rail has the potential to increase travel quality. The means to achieve this increase are higher frequencies, more comfort brought about by new vehicles, and upgrading of stops. The door-to-door travel time is reduced due to having more stops than regular rail connections and the new vehicles. The so-called rail bonus and higher reliability are also included in the discussion. Mobility reliability has become more important over the years and, similarly, reliability is an important aspect of quality in public transport, too. Both travellers and operators benefit from reliable travel times, brought about by shorter and more predictable trips, as well as lower costs. However, there is not much good (quantitative) evidence to support this claim. In this chapter we would like to present this support. Light rail has the aforementioned potential, that is, if designed properly. In this chapter we will present quantitative research on both rail bonus and reliability. We will use the *RandstadRail* case to illustrate the possibilities to increase reliability at a strategic level (network design) and a tactical level (timetable). More details may be found in Van Oort and van Nes (2009a,b), Van Oort et al. (2015) and Bunschoten et al. (2012).

5.1 RAIL BONUS

Since light rail requires considerably larger financial investments than a bus line, its implementation must be thought through very carefully. It is relevant to wonder if there is such a thing as a rail bonus or a tram bonus. These bonuses would be the added value causing more travellers to use light rail rather than bus, when a bus line is converted into a light rail connection. Some experts in the field are convinced there is such a thing as rail bonus, even though no explanation for this phenomenon can be given. Others claim that bus and light rail are comparable means of transport.

The literature is unclear on the matter of rail bonus. In particular, German researchers like Husler, Arnold, and Lohrmann and Kasch and

Light Rail Transit Systems
ISBN 978-0-12-814784-9
https://doi.org/10.1016/B978-0-12-814784-9.00005-0

Vogts studied the number of travellers before and after rail implementation. Their results showed different rates of passenger increase: from 15% to 54%. These studies did not solely cover traveller increase caused by change of means of transport; there were other network changes involved, such as tunnels stretching several kilometres or the construction of a complete network of rail lines. Other aspects that ought to be considered when comparing the numbers of travellers before and after rail implementation are spatial planning and time frame. Both situations are difficult to compare, because full realization can takes years.

Several studies on rail bonus based on models show that travellers prefer public transport on rail, although they give no clear explanation as to why. Since in most studies more parameters are changed than solely bus lines being replaced with rail lines, it is difficult to tell whether changes in the numbers of travellers are caused by a distinctive preference for light rail compared to bus. This is why it is still unclear if there is such a thing as rail bonus, how significant it would be and what it is connected with. To answer these questions a choice experiment was conducted amongst inhabitants of large cities in the Netherlands. Respondents were recruited in cities both with and without urban rail. The choice experiment required respondents to choose between a bus alternative and a rail alternative. Both alternatives differ in the same aspects, therefore the difference in mode-specific constant indicates the difference in preference. The perceptions of a number of mode characteristics of bus and light rail were measured to explain the difference in preference. Finally, the transition from difference in preference to the number of travellers was made using a traffic model.

The effect of preference on a percentage of extra travellers was determined using elasticities in the traffic model and perceived travel times. The ratio between parameters of travel time by tram and travel time by bus determines the perceived travel times. This is shown in Table 5.1.

The ratio indicates that when a minute travelled by bus is valued as 1 min, this minute in light rail is valued as 47 s (60 × 0.78). Travelling by light rail is therefore perceived as shorter than travelling by bus. This perception is taken into account for the implementation of the preference

Table 5.1 Parameter Values of Bus and Light Rail

Parameter	Value	Value
Bus	−0.0804	1
Light rail	−0.0628	0.78

of urban rail in a traffic model. To this end, the VRU model was used. This model was developed by the regional transit authority and includes the new light rail line to the Uithof, where the university campus and several businesses are located. The actual travel time of the *Uithof line* by bus is used as the reference framework. Travellers are assigned to the network. Then the travel time of the *Uithof line* by rail was multiplied by 0.78, which results in the so-called perceived travel time. With an elasticity of −1.0 (meaning that a 1% gain in travel time results in 1% more travellers) traffic is reassigned again for the entire network. The proposed change from bus to rail resulted in the prospect of an increase in travellers of 4.3%.

Judging from the model it can be concluded that in most cases light rail is preferred to bus. This means there is a positive preference for rail compared to the bus, and the atmosphere in the vehicle, vehicle characteristics, and display of travel information account for this. Differences in preference will be large if these aspects differ greatly between modes of transport. However, if they differ only slightly the perception of the modes will be similar, resulting in little difference in preference. This can mean that a bus can be upgraded to 'rail level' to receive a positive preference compared to a bus that was not upgraded.

5.2 RELIABILITY

Being able to offer a more reliable public transport service is an added value of light rail. Reliability is defined as how certain it is that a service is performed, as perceived by the traveller. It is one of the most important characteristics of the quality of the public transport product.

Fig. 5.1, which is based on research by Brons and Rietveld from 2007, shows that travellers find reliability important, but they rate it as unsatisfactory. Table 5.2 (Vrije Universiteit, 1998) shows how travellers adjust their itinerary when reliability increases. These results show that mainly incidental travellers start travelling more by public transport at a higher reliability (44%).

Reliability is a major component of the customer requirements pyramid. The Dutch Railways (NS; Van Hagen, 2011) developed this pyramid to convey the perception of public transport (Fig. 5.2). Qualities that travellers require to be primarily in order are at the bottom of the pyramid. This is where we find reliability (and safety), which means it is a primary condition of quality for public transport use. In addition to this, a public transport trip must be fast enough to compete with other modes of transport.

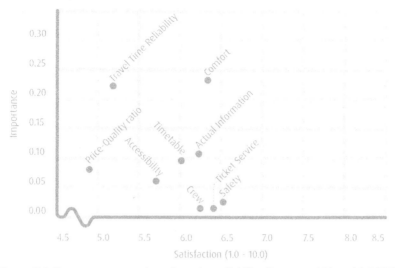

Figure 5.1 Passenger perception of service reliability (Brons and Rietveld, 2007).

Table 5.2 Effects of Changes in Unreliability (Standard Deviation of Travel Time) on Mode Choice (Vrije Universiteit, 1998)

Travellers' Change of Unreliability	Regular Travellers	Occasional Travellers	Non-Travellers
Decrease	9%[a]	22%[a]	9%[a]
Increase	17%[b]	44%[b]	—

[a]Travellers that will travel more often by public transport.
[b]Travellers that will travel less often by public transport.

Figure 5.2 Customer requirements pyramid (Van Hagen, 2011).

Presently attention to reliability and its improvement is mainly given at an operational level. The perception we have is that only little attention is given to this aspect of quality during public transport planning. The only things that have a positive influence on reliability that are explicitly taken into consideration when the network is designed are priority at traffic lights and separate lanes. At the moment reliability is considered from the perspective of the vehicle: is the train or bus late? Though this is important, it is more important whether the traveller is on time or not. Unreliability has three important effects on the traveller. These are extension of average travel time, variation in average travel time, and decrease in both comfort and a chance of a seat in the vehicle. We will give an example of a situation where light rail provides the traveller with more reliability.

5.3 LIGHT RAIL IN PRACTICE (CASE *RANDSTADRAIL*, NETHERLANDS)

We will now describe the possibilities for enhancing reliability on a strategic and a tactical level: the design of the network and the timetable, respectively. A great deal of attention in the literature is given to enhancing reliability at an operational level, while there are also possibilities at planning levels. Both approaches are combined here to achieve an optimally reliable public transport system and there is a follow-up to our prior research.

The control philosophy that was proposed in this earlier study has since been refined and, in addition to this, the first results from the field are now available. These are also presented here. We conducted this research using the *RandstadRail* case. *RandstadRail* is the light rail system that was introduced in 2007 in the urban area of The Hague and Rotterdam, often called 'Zuidvleugel' (South Wing) or Metropolitan region Rotterdam The Hague (MRDH, Metropoolregio Rotterdam Den Haag).

RandstadRail offers high-quality public transport. Services on the entire network are highly frequent and performed quickly, comfortably and reliably. *RandstadRail* replaces and connects former tramways, metro lines and railways. It contains two rail networks. Tramways 3 and 6 in The Hague are connected with the former Zoetermeer line (the rail line between The Hague and Zoetermeer).

HTM operates the services on these lines. The secondary rail line between The Hague and Rotterdam (the so-called Hofplein line) is intertwined with the Rotterdam metro. Service on this line is operated by RET.

Figure 5.3 *RandstadRail* network.

We limited our case to The Hague part of *RandstadRail*: lines RR3 and RR4 (Fig. 5.3). The former mainly follows the route of the old line 3 in The Hague; the latter also uses adjusted tram routes, with an added newly built route, and partly follows the route of the old line 6. To some extent both lines have their own routes in Zoetermeer. The *RandstadRail* project RR4 was extended on a new, elevated track.

Prior to *RandstadRail*, public transport in The Hague was not controlled or dispatched very delicately. Drivers knew the arrival and departure times on their lines. During the trip there were gradual disruptions, causing variations to travel times.

The variation of these lines has been analysed extensively, including old tram lines 3 and 6, which were later converted into *RandstadRail*. This research shows that a variation of approximately 3 min at the point of departure can increase to approximately 10 min in the town centre.

When *RandstadRail* was initiated the network included two lines between Zoetermeer and The Hague and both had a frequency of 12 times per hour in peak hours. This entailed a 2.5-min service on the route where both lines ran. High frequencies like this are not feasible when variation increases to 10 min. There are two reasons why these deviations should be minimized.

First off, high punctuality. Offering high quality is of the utmost importance. The chances of obtaining seats are optimal when travellers are divided equally amongst the vehicles at high-frequency lines of public transport with a uniform passenger-arrival time at stops. In addition to this, the wait time at a stop is minimal when the public transport service is regular.

The second reason why travel-time spread should be minimized is to prevent congestion on the tracks. These tailbacks cause service irregularities. Security measures are in force at parts of *RandstadRail*, limiting capacity compared to a situation without security. The total planned frequency of all lines (tram and *RandstadRail*) is about 40 vehicles per direction per hour on the busiest part of the track. Capacity is sufficient, assuming a regular pattern of vehicle arrival. Disturbance in regularity will cause rail congestion and, consequently, delays.

Accumulation of vehicles must be prevented. To do so, attention must be paid to preventing deviation from the established timetable, as well as limiting its effects. *RandstadRail* is a regional public transport system with high reliability. The government body in charge of *RandstadRail* is very demanding when it comes to guaranteeing this. The requirements for reliability are expressed as a maximum number of trips. Ideally, 0% of trips are early, while a maximum of 5% of all trips have a delay of over 2 min. Finally, only 1% of all trips can have a delay of over 4 min. These objectives are not met without extra measures, taking into account the tram deviations presented here and the planned high frequencies. This is why a control philosophy is necessary which meets maximal percentages on both the planning and operational levels. This control philosophy is drawn up as a set of measures. As was pointed out earlier, variation in travel time and timetable deviations should be prevented. HTM, the operator, has designed a three-step control philosophy to achieve this (Fig. 5.4).

Preventing **disruptions** is the first and most important step. There are several ways to prevent **spread**. The following adjustments have been made for *RandstadRail*:

Infrastructural improvements − Infrastructure is an important cause of variation. *RandstadRail* actually consists of two parts: former tram routes and former train routes. The latter function independently from all other traffic,

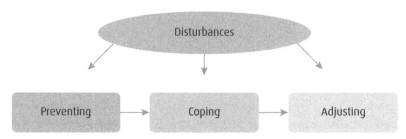

Figure 5.4 Three-step control philosophy.

while the former contain crossings. A major part of the infrastructure has been improved for *RandstadRail*, resulting in more separate lanes, fewer crossings, and greater priority at traffic lights.

Up-to-date punctuality information for the driver — Information on punctuality is shown to the driver to increase awareness of the importance of timeliness and to help them drive on time. An example display is shown in Fig. 5.5.

Timely departure — Departure punctuality was not high prior to the introduction of *RandstadRail*, neither was on-route punctuality. In order to achieve high punctuality, large variation at the point of departure is unacceptable. Departure punctuality depends on three major factors, all of which have been improved for *RandstadRail*. The first factor is the presence of the vehicle at the point of departure. To achieve this, there needs to be sufficient time for driving and turning the vehicle. Secondly, the driver needs to be at the departure stop on time. When a *RandstadRail* driver does not log in on time, central traffic control is warned so that

Figure 5.5 Delays are displayed in quarters of minutes with a background colour indicating the type of delay (ahead or too late). This information supports the driver to achieve high schedule adherence by departing on time and preventing driving ahead of schedule.

appropriate measures can be taken. Finally, punctuality is constantly monitored and made public.

RandstadRail is not supposed to depart early from the stop. Being early creates variation in travel times and thus accumulation of vehicles. This reduces quality: longer wait times and less chance of seats being available for travellers. When a vehicle arrives at its stop early, its stationary time should be extended. However, this extension is only short, because the timetable is strict and the vehicle did not leave its previous stop prematurely.

Though punctuality is a much-used indicator for reliability, it is not the best conveyor of reliability. Additional wait time is a better indicator for travellers to assess reliability. This is subject to calculation (see Table 5.3). The effect not departing early has on punctuality and additional wait time has been calculated for all tram lines in The Hague in a case study. Actual data about travellers and travel times were used as input. Table 5.3 shows the results for line 6, which was transformed into *RandstadRail*. The results show that a major increase in punctuality is to be expected if departures are neither early, nor late. It is expected that the effect on additional wait times is even greater. Travellers on this line will experience 40% less additional wait time as a consequence of reduced variation in travel times. Table 5.3 shows the example of line 6 and the anticipated effects of the measures regarding punctuality and additional wait time.

New stopping process — Not only infrastructure can cause variation. Stopping can also be a cause. Some variation can be prevented by introducing several measures.

Conventional trams will skip stops if there are no passengers to board or alight, but *RandstadRail* trains stop at every stop, just like regular trains do. Fig. 5.6 illustrates the distribution of the total stop time on line 1. The variation turns out to be large. This will decrease when fixed stop times are introduced. Stopping at every stop will cause a reduction in average speed, but this is outweighed by higher reliability. The second measure concerns the vehicles. *RandstadRail* only uses the latest state-of-the-art vehicles

Table 5.3 Potential Improvements

	Punctuality (min)	Average Additional Waiting Time (s)
Current tram	1.9	80
Departure punctuality	1.6	60
Departure punctuality optimal	1.4	50

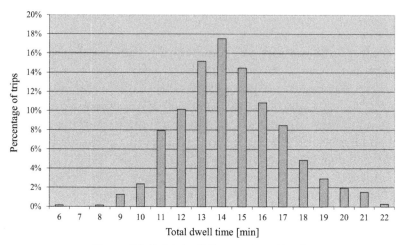

Figure 5.6 Total dwell time on tram line 1.

whose entrances are at the same level as the platform, enabling stops to proceed smoothly. In addition to this, stops have been made wider and more accessible. The fourth measure involves the driver no longer being responsible for sales and information distribution. These tasks are now carried out by ticket machines and an on-board information channel, respectively.

New planning process — RandstadRail is a hybrid public transport system with characteristics of both trains and trams. The planning process should be adjusted accordingly. Major changes are planning with an accuracy of 15 s, a comparison with the theoretically feasible travel time, and planning the timetable from stop to stop.

Fig. 5.7 shows the expected effects of all aforementioned measures. The black lines show the present travel-time variation, which will be reduced by improving both infrastructure and vehicles (white line). The increase in punctuality at the first stop and the prevention of early departure will help decrease variation even further (grey line).

The second step in the control philosophy is handling delays: using time buffers to absorb delays. These buffers can be included in travel times, stop times, and turn times. Small disruptions can be handled this way. What is important, when it comes to buffers, is their duration and location. When implementing buffers, it is important to take into consideration the interests

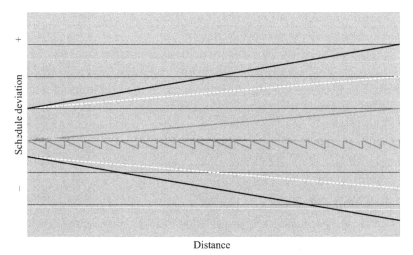

Figure 5.7 Expected impacts control philosophy on trip time distribution. *Black lines* shows noncontrolled distribution; *white line* after set of infrastructure measures; *grey lines* after preventing early departures as well.

of both through travellers and travellers at the next stops. Buffers that were not used are a nuisance to through travellers (because the vehicle is early and has to wait), but buffers do benefit travellers at the next stops, who will have less additional wait time, since the service is punctual and regular.

Some extra scheduled time allows delayed vehicles to catch up, but causes delays for punctual vehicles. Speed and reliability must be considered here. Most buffer time should be part of the vehicle turn time. This allows for it to start the return journey without presenting passengers with additional travel time.

Even after steps A and B delays can still occur, in which case step C is taken. Step C is adjusting operations, which is done by central traffic controllers. They have an overview of all vehicles on the lines and their corresponding punctuality. There are software tools to both adjust exploitation and inform drivers and travellers automatically.

The main goal of adjusting operations is punctuality. The system warns traffic controllers when punctuality exceeds certain limits, possibly caused by delayed drivers, defect vehicles, and early or delayed departures from stops. Several measures can be taken, like shortening a trip or line, adding another vehicle, or skipping stops to make up for lost time. These measures are always taken after considering the needs of both passengers in the vehicle and passengers waiting at a stop. Which measure is taken depends on the outcome of the analysis of the effects.

The second goal of adjusting operations is maintaining regularity. If punctuality is badly disrupted, regularity adjusting operations can be applied. This involves slowing down vehicles in the proximity of a delayed vehicle in order to restore regularity and increase reliability, which results in less additional wait time and therefore a shorter travel time. It also brings about a better distribution of passengers across the vehicles, increasing the chances of a seat.

Calculating Travellers

Indicators like punctuality and regularity are used to measure the extent of public transport's reliability. However, these indicators only address performances by vehicles and do not say anything about the effects on travellers. In order to get a more complete view on these effects TU Delft (Van Oort, 2011) developed a traveller-oriented indicator: the extra travel time caused by unreliability as perceived by travellers.

When calculating this extra travel time distinction must be made between high-frequency systems (which involve passengers arriving randomly at the stop) and low-frequency systems (which involve passengers planning their arrival at the stop). Punctuality is not very important in high-frequency situations, because travellers do not pay attention to the timetable. The extra wait time is determined by the extent to which the sequence of vehicles is constant. The larger the variation in sequence, the larger the average wait time for travellers.

This can be calculated using the following formula:

$$T^{wait} = \frac{H}{2} \times \left(1 + CoV^2(H)\right)$$

where T^{wait} is the average wait time for travellers, H (headway) is the time between vehicles and CoV (H) is the variation. If variation is 0 and vehicles show up regularly, CoV (H) is zero. As a consequence the formula dictates that the average wait time is $H/2$, half the headway. As soon as the variation in headway increases (and regularity decreases) wait time increases exponentially. In the case of 'bunching', also known as the accordion effect, the average wait will double to an entire headway. This means that the average wait time for a 10-min service will not be 5 min, but 10.

Calculating Travellers—cont'd

Travellers use timetables to plan their arrival at a stop in the case of low-frequency systems. This results in a different method of calculation; the corresponding formula can be found below. It can be assumed that the difference between a traveller's arrival and the planned departure time is τ_{early}, a safety margin for the planned departure time. It is stated that the traveller does not experience extra wait time if the vehicle departs between τ_{early} and a small, acceptable margin after planned departure time τ_{late}. The effect on travellers of a vehicle being early is very different from the effect of being delayed, because an early departure (that is, more than τ_{early}) has travellers wait an entire headway (H; assuming the next vehicle departs on time). This can lead to very long extra wait times in low frequencies. Imagine a 30-min service and the vehicle having already left before you arrived at the stop. In case of a late departure (more than τ_{late}) the extra wait time equals the delay of the vehicle (d). This way of calculating is included below in the form of a formula.

$$\begin{cases} T^{extra} = H & als & d \leq -\tau_{early} \\ T^{extra} = 0 & als & -\tau_{early} < d < \tau_{late} \\ T^{extra} = d & als & d \geq \tau_{late} \end{cases}$$

The comparisons in this frame text have been simplified. They can be found in their complete forms in Van Oort (2011).

Waiting passengers at tram stop, Paris *T1*, Courneuve.

5.4 LIGHT RAIL IN PRACTICE, PART 2

The previous section featured the control philosophy as was applied in the Hague part of *RandstadRail*. The aim was to achieve higher levels of quality and reliability. Now we will show how the level of reliability developed in the years after the introduction in 2007. We used the *RandstadRail* case to monitor the actual effects of the control measures.

Punctuality — the control philosophy states that the departure from the first stop is significant. Drivers must not be early. *RandstadRail* departure punctuality at first stops has increased in comparison to the situation before. The number of vehicles that leave within −1 and +1 min has gone up from 70% to 93%.

RandstadRail does not permit early departure. A display in the driver's compartment shows punctuality, so s/he can adjust their behaviour accordingly. Travel times are planned shorter than usual in urban public transport. The number of trips that depart early has gone down from 50% to 6.5% after the introduction of this measure.

Variation in travel times — two major causes for variation in travel times are stopping at stops and stopping at other places than stops (e.g., at traffic lights). Previous research has shown that the variation in these elements leads to a larger variation in travel times. This is why it is necessary to contain variation in both elements to ultimately obtain a smaller variation in travel times.

RandstadRail has brought about infrastructure improvements. Stopping at places that are not actual stops must be prevented as much as possible in order to achieve a high level of quality. Infrastructure has been improved to this end: more separate lanes and greater priority at traffic lights. Table 5.4 shows the average delay per trip on a route both before and after the introduction of *RandstadRail*. Results include a decreased average value and also a reduced standard deviation, resulting in more reliable service operation.

Secondly, vehicles have been improved substantially. The greatest advantage of the new *RandstadRail* vehicles is the low floor. Boarding and alighting have become much easier, especially for the elderly and people with trolleys and luggage. This prevents excesses in stop time. Fig. 5.8 shows the standard deviation of the stop time per stop before and after the transition to *RandstadRail*.

Standard deviation has decreased at most stops. Table 5.5 shows that standard deviation decreased from 20 to 7 s. The average stop time has been reduced from 28 to 24 s. This improvement facilitates a reliable service.

Table 5.4 Potential Improvements

	Punctuality (min)	Average Additional Waiting Time (s)
Current tram	1.9	80
Departure punctuality	1.6	60
Departure punctuality optimal	1.4	50

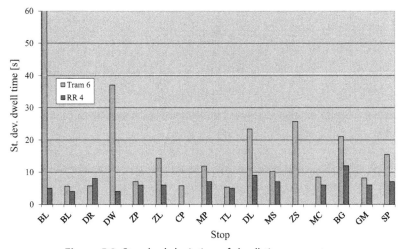

Figure 5.8 Standard deviation of dwell times per stop.

Table 5.5 Average Dwell Time and Variation on the Line

	Average Dwell Time (s)	Average Standard Deviation (s)
Tram	28	20
RandstadRail	24	7

Variation of stop time at an individual stop. Fig. 5.9 shows that excesses in stop times have decreased, in particular due to a better boarding and alighting process.

Total effect control — The aim of control philosophy is improving the level of reliability by limiting the variation in vehicles and improving punctuality. Fig. 5.10 shows 15 and 85 percentile values of the travel time of line 6 before and after applying control philosophy. Variation decreased and punctuality improved, as had been expected. The deviation is smaller and the negative delays are almost gone. This has resulted in higher traveller appreciation (see Fig. 5.11).

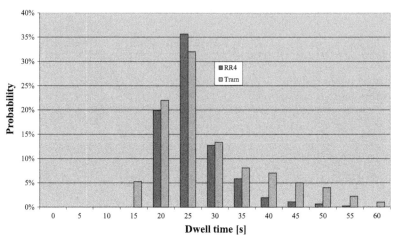

Figure 5.9 Distribution of dwell times before (tram) and after (RR4) the introduction of light rail.

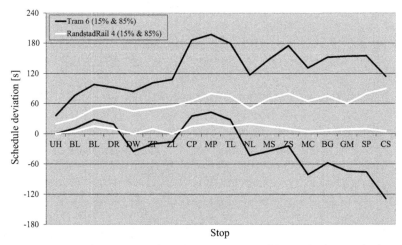

Figure 5.10 15- and 85 percentile values trip times of line 6 before and after the introduction of *RandstadRail*.

To conclude, *RandstadRail* is a light rail line in the The Hague area that replaced and connects two tramways and a railway. It is a high-quality public transport system with high frequencies and shared routes with tram and metro. The decision was made to apply control philosophy to

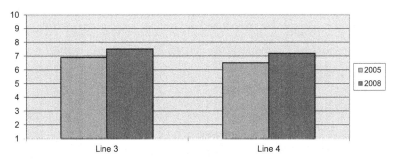

Figure 5.11 Customer satisfaction before (2005) and after (2008) the introduction of light rail on lines 3 and 4.

offer high quality in terms of punctuality, regularity and efficient use of the infrastructure. Important aspects of this are the prevention, absorption and redirecting of variation and exploitation, respectively. A display in the driver's compartment shows punctuality, so the driver can adjust their actions according to the timetable. Central traffic control keeps an eye on all vehicles and their punctuality. Service operation can be redirected in case of disruptions. *RandstadRail* often has its own, separate lane and priority at traffic lights. The vehicles have wide doors and offer entry at platform level, which influences the stopping process in a positive way.

RandstadRail offers a highly reliable service, here at one of the Souterrain stations in The Hague centre.

After *RandstadRail* had started, all measures from control philosophy were analysed using up-to-date service information. It turns out that variation in travel time decreased compared to the previous situation and punctuality increased. Higher reliability reduced average travel time. Improved regularity increased the chances of a seat, while insecurity amongst travellers was decreased.

Serving *RandstadRail*

Kees Pronk is tram driver and loves riding *RandstadRail*.

Reliability, punctuality and comfort are important characteristics of our case *RandstadRail*, the cutting-edge light rail project in the urban southwest of the Netherlands. Our conversation with tram driver Kees Pronk exposes his daily practice. Since 2013 former computer professional Mr. Pronk has been a motivated driver serving *RandstadRail* and various tram lines in the urban region of The Hague (the latter operated with the new Avenio cars). In addition, he is a well-known Dutch tramway connoisseur. We appreciate his permission for use of some of his images in this book.

'I like my work very much', he says, 'driving Alstom LRVs of *RandstadRail* is engaging. Moreover operator HTM is a nice company to work for. For instance, they had prepared breakfast on my first time *RandstadRail* duty during Christmas. Or when announcing myself at the yard of the depot "Hi Kees" is always there, because they know you. It gives me a good feeling'.

'The lines of *RandstadRail* are pretty long (RR3 33.4 km, RR4 29.6 km). I never serve these lines more than twice or three times during one duty. For example RR3, takes over an hour to run from one end to the other. One lap including rest easily covers two and a half hour. Serving regional *RandstadRail* is much more varied compared with working shorter city lines'.

'*RandstadRail* drivers get a special five week training. My first time running a vehicle at the regional infrastructure was not easy to get used to. You have to learn all routes thoroughly. Also, handling of all equipment is subject to training.

Serving *RandstadRail*—cont'd

In particular, you gain experience with difficult traffic situations, with emergency stops and, for instance, with common malfunctions of the LRV'.

'When you have passed your exam you're scheduled for regular services, with passengers. During the first 2 weeks you are guided by an instructor who eventually assesses and reports on your work progress. If everything is okay than you have it and you will go on the tracks without any assistance. At first serving alone is a bit strange. Yet after a couple of days you're accustomed to.'

Security

ZUB-loop at right side of track.

Kees Pronk et al. drive by sight when *RandstadRail* routes coincide with the existing urban tramway network. At tunnel sections (e.g., the 'Souterrain') and elevated sections of that network (e.g., the famous landmark '*Netkous*', i.e., 'Fishnet Stocking') all drivers are backed by a simple security system, called 'automatic brake interference' (ARI).

From the beginning of the former heavy rail section, *RandstadRail* has been secured with a train control system called ZUB (German for '*Zugbeeinflussung*'). This system is supplied by Siemens and utilizes loops (technically induction coils) along the right side of the track. *RandstadRail* is equipped with 'ZUB 222c' type that serves drivers with information on signalling images and takes care of automatic security. Besides this, 222c-type allows the operation of switches from the LRVs and also communication with Central Traffic Control (CVL) to ask permission to drive on.

In our conversation Kees Pronk emphasizes the big difference between classic urban tramways that force him to allow for other traffic and the former heavy railways that offer him a ride with his LRV on a fully separated

Continued

Serving *RandstadRail*—cont'd

Infrastructure. On the latter, driving conditions are ruled by ZUB, he explains. 'If a signal shows green you always can drive on. If a signal is displaying red, and the previous signal was yellow, then I had to reduce my speed sufficiently in order to make my stop in due time at the upcoming red signal. The ZUB-system watches if I did reduce my speed appropriately. However, in the meantime the red signal could have been switched to yellow or green. In that case you wouldn't have had to reduce speed. Fortunately, additional loops in between two signals provide you with changed signalling. So, in this way you can make use of the improved signalling image. At first *RandstadRail* was not equipped with additional loops halfway and a lot of time was lost. It caused unnecessary delays. Certainly, on the busy shared section where our LRVs and those of the Rotterdam service make use of the same tracks'.

'As a matter of fact, compared to ZUB the ARI-system at tunnel and elevated sections in The Hague city is less effective. In the case of ignoring red signalling, or a disturbance occurring, ARI abruptly triggers the brake interference. Your LRV is stopped at once, just because ARI, so to say, has provoked a real emergency break. This is not very comfortable and safe for passengers. In such a case the driver certainly must check whether any passengers have fallen or been hurt'.

Reliability

'Over the last few years *RandstadRail's* reliability has been improved. There are less disturbances and LRVs are on time more often', underlines Kees Pronk. 'Moreover, punctuality is monitored accurately and precisely. As a driver you're subjected to a yearly performance review. Your way of driving and particularly your achieved punctuality are the subject of conversation. If necessary every trip can be traced and scrutinized in detail'.

For Mr. Pronk, being a tram driver, it's obvious that he needs to depart at every stop right on time, hence, not too early nor too late. 'The display in front of my cabin comes in handy when I have to verify my departure time. In theory I depart when my display is showing zero. However, the actual departure time has to be 15 s later. It took a while before I was accustomed to this. If I understand correctly, these 15 s are necessary to prevent my departure being marked by satellite as "to early". Confusing! Anyway, again, I'm always taking care to depart right on time. Except in special cases, for instance, when an old lady with a walker enters the platform'.

Software can affect reliability. The new generation of LRVs, like the Alstom vehicles of *RandstadRail* are computer-controlled. Kees Pronk's experience showed the sensitivity of their computer system. 'For example, when an LRV has been switched off at night (e.g., when overhead wire work was necessary) the following morning it sometimes can't be started up due to the cold. Fortunately usually everything is all right, though occasionally it takes a pretty long time before the computer system has been started up. And you need the system for

Serving *RandstadRail*—cont'd

setting your route and corresponding codes. Technically you're able to drive your LRV without its computer system being in operation. However, in such a case you need to consult Central Traffic Control (CVL) first, otherwise switches on your route can't be set in the right position. Moreover, your route codes are necessary for communication with CVL and monitoring of your trip by CVL'.

Over and above software, hardware can also affect reliability. *RandstadRail's* hardware entails LRVs and infrastructure. Fortunately, over the last years the quality of both has been raised to an adequate level. However, as Dutch tramway connoisseur Kees Pronk noticed, fairly longer times for door opening and closing are required for his LRV compared to the simple and fast doors of a vintage tram vehicle, i.e., the American-based PCC who acquired The Hague as one the first cities in Europe during the post-war period. Nevertheless, getting in and out is much faster than previously due to the similar heights of the platform and vehicle floor.

Another hardware issue Kees Pronk emphasizes is the limited opportunity for diversion of *RandstadRail* in the case of accidents, despite the availability of protocols when blocks appear. As a tram driver this irritates him sometimes as most disruptions happen in the city. Delays and disruptions are less common in the urban region on the former heavy rail network and are mostly due to signal or switch malfunctions. 'Though these disruptions are rare ordinary driving prevails', says Kees Pronk. Therefore, regularity and reliability are typical for daily operation experienced from his cabin. Even during busy rush hours there is normally no 'caking' of LRVs.

Kees Pronk: 'You must always tell passengers what's going on'.

Continued

Serving *RandstadRail*—cont'd

Yet again says Kees Pronk: 'if there's any disturbance I like to make an announcement. Once I had a journey that was delayed due to every signal improperly showing red. Then I announced to my passengers "there is one consolation for you all, I'm also gong to be late getting home". This is the way you should act as tram driver. If you say nothing, you shouldn't be surprised when passengers become annoyed or even angry. You always must tell passengers what's going on'.

CHAPTER 6

Costs—Benefits of Light Rail Revised

As Chapter 5 showed, reliability is an important quality aspect of high-quality public transport systems, like light rail. Light rail can bring about a substantial improvement in reliability. A solid set of considerations is necessary to compare the investments and benefits. What is surprising, though, is that the societal cost—benefit analyses (SCBAs) pay little explicit attention to the benefits of more reliable public transport. Though the SCBA guidelines mention public transport reliability as a possible benefit, there are no tools for a structural approach. Fig. 6.1 shows the results of a quick scan of incorporating reliability effects in more than 25 recent and randomly selected public transport projects in the Netherlands, with which a representative picture can be painted (Van Oort, 2016). This illustration shows that explicit incorporation of these benefits happens only to a very limited extent. If benefits are mentioned at all, it only happens based on a qualitative estimation of expert judgement. More details may be found in Van Oort (2016).

The conclusion that attention to reliability is only limited can also be drawn from many other studies. Only a limited number of countries, like the United Kingdom, the Netherlands, Denmark, New Zealand, Australia, Norway and Sweden take it explicitly into account. Nowadays, the US and Germany can be included in this list. However, most applications are aimed at car traffic and not public transport.

One of the reasons not to include public transport reliability benefits is the complexity of the calculations and data needs. The focus is on vehicle reliability and not, like in SCBAs, on travellers. In this chapter we will show that it is possible to map reliability benefits quantitatively. We will use a case study to show that the effects can be significant.

We have developed a method to calculate reliability benefits and include them in an SCBA thanks to the present availability of data, both on vehicles and travellers, combined with scientific insights. The structure of the chapter is as follows: traveller effects of public transport unreliability are

Light Rail Transit Systems
ISBN 978-0-12-814784-9
https://doi.org/10.1016/B978-0-12-814784-9.00006-2

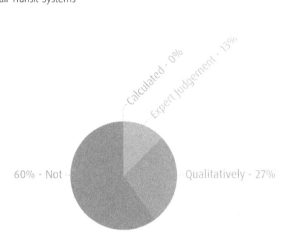

Figure 6.1 Results survey service reliability in CBAs.

described in the first section. We will present our approach to include these effects quantitatively in SCBAs in the second section. In the third section we will illustrate our approach using the *Uithof line* case study.

6.1 EFFECTS OF RELIABILITY ON TRAVELLERS

Research shows that public transport reliability influences several choices, like mode and route. The three main effects of unreliability are longer average travel time, deviation in time of arrival, and more crowded vehicles. All three of these effects should be included in an SCBA. In this chapter we will only examine the effects on travel time.

Research shows that the essence of calculating traveller effects of unreliable public transport is the transition of vehicle effects to travellers. Punctuality and regularity, the usual public transport reliability indicators, do not (fully) cover traveller effects. These indicators are aimed more at variation in the supply. Though this is related to traveller effects, there is no straightforward transition. Leaving 3 min early, for instance, tends to have bigger consequences than leaving 3 min late. Punctuality no longer matters in case of high frequencies. We have developed a new reliability standard to handle this shortcoming of public transport indicators. This standard, the additional average travel time per traveller, indicates how much travel time increases when service operation deviates from the planned timetable. This is the origin of including reliability benefits in SCBAs. In addition to the absolute value, the average additional travel time, this is also about the variation in travel time that results from unreliable public transport.

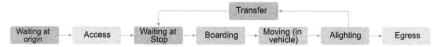

Figure 6.2 Passenger travel time components.

Travellers will experience no additional travel time if a service is operated exactly according to the timetable. Their total travel time consists of access and egress, wait time at the stop, and in-vehicle time, as illustrated in Fig. 6.2. In some cases there is also transfer time.

Should a traveller arrive at a stop at a random moment, the wait time is not fixed, but uniformly divided between 0 and the interval time. On average, the wait time is therefore half the interval time for a 100% reliable operation. Random arrivals tend to occur at high frequencies, that is, intervals of 10 min or less. Based on a traveller survey in The Hague we concluded that this 10-min interval is when most travellers stop using a timetable and randomly go to a stop instead. This is in line with previous research in this field. Wait time is fixed when travellers know the departure time and adjust their arrival accordingly (assuming service is operated punctually). Fig. 6.3 shows how the moment of arrival is divided amongst travellers, based on a traveller survey in The Hague.

As soon as there is variation in service operation there will be consequences for both wait time and in-vehicle time. The effect on wait time depends on travellers' pattern of arrival, as well as the (lack of) regularity and punctuality of the vehicles. Supposed connection time is influenced by variation in supply, like late arrival, causing the passenger to miss a connecting vehicle.

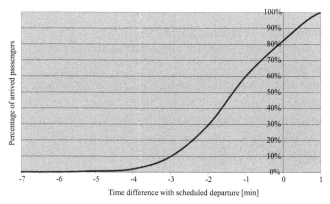

Figure 6.3 Arrival pattern of passengers at the first stop.

Variation in travel times and therefore headway at stops prolongs the average wait time, and thus total travel time. The access and egress times do not change if the choice of stop remains the same. The in-vehicle time is also influenced by variation in travel times, but the effect differs for each traveller. This effect depends on choices in the timetable design. If the average value of travel time is used for the timetable and if different periods have an equal division of travel times, some travellers will have longer in-vehicle times and others will have shorter in-vehicle times than average. On average the in-vehicle time will be the same as planned, unless vehicles are rescheduled, for example, to prevent early departure. To find out the extent of the additional travel time effects for all travellers, individual trips are used to calculate the average. The correlation between wait time and irregularity is expanded on in Section 6.2.

A fictional example of a PT line is given below to indicate what the effect of an irregular service operation is. The example states a 10-min wait time at a stop. If the service is operated regularly, a vehicle will depart every 5 min. Passengers arrive at the stop at random moments (equally divided in time). Two hundred travellers depart every 10 min. The red line in Fig. 6.4 indicates the pattern of the number of waiting travellers that emerges over time in a regularly operated service.

The pattern is no longer regular if operations are disturbed. In this example the first vehicle arrives 2.5 min late, so after 7.5 min instead of after 5 min. The second vehicle does arrive on time (after 10 min). The pattern of this irregular service operation in correlation with the number of travellers waiting is included in Fig. 6.4 by means of the yellow dotted line.

Hindrance for travellers can now be expressed by determining the wait time for all 200 travellers and using it to calculate the average. It is possible to determine the total wait time using the surface below the graph (number of travellers waiting × wait time/traveller), because travellers arrived at the stop at steady intervals. The figure below shows the values of these surfaces until a vehicle departs.

By adding up the surfaces of the regular and irregular service operation for the examined 10 min and dividing them by the total number of travellers in the same period, an indication of the average wait time emerges (Table 6.1). This shows that irregular service operation enhances the average wait time for travellers.

The advantage of the use of the above-presented values for unreliability is that the focus moves from vehicles to travellers. As a consequence, the effects of some choices in network and timetable designs can be tested for

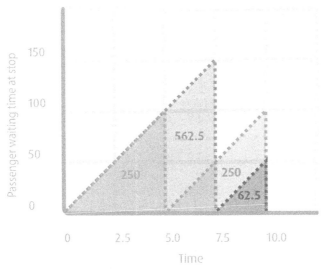

Figure 6.4 Number of waiting passengers.

effects on travellers immediately. Because of its focus on travellers, this value is very suitable in SCBAs, which was not possible until recently. Another advantage of this indictor is that the trade-off between speed and reliability is easy to map. Both are expressed as time effects. Sometimes measures improve reliability, but not speed, like the time buffers included in the timetable. Sole focus on vehicle reliability may cause the time buffer in the timetable to grow too large, resulting in a service operation that is punctual, but with longer travel times.

The average additional travel time per PT traveller is a new value in both science and practice. International research shows that the government organization Transport for London (TfL) is alone in employing a similar indicator, called the excess journey time. This indicator also applies to additional travel time as a consequence of unreliable service operation, but compares it with the free flow, instead of planned travel time. An application of Van Oort's (2011) indicator in SCBAs is given in this chapter.

Table 6.1 Impacts of Irregular/Regular Services

(*) 200 Passengers	Total Waiting Times* (min)	(*) 200 Passengers Average Waiting Time (min)
Regular operations	500	2.5
Irregular operations	625	3.1

Not only does unreliable service operation cause additional travel time, it also causes variation in travel time in general. Travel times will always be the same in a system that is 100% reliable. If there are incidental disruptions the total travel time will be different each time and travellers' arrival times will also depend on coincidence. There is additional travel time, but no variation if the disruptions are the same every time. It makes sense in this rare case to resort to timetable adjustments. There are several values described in the literature that express variation in travel time, like differences in percentile value and standard deviation. The reliability buffer time (RBT) was developed to this end. This is the difference between the 95th and the 50th percentile values. If commuters incorporated this buffer in their planning they would arrive late for work only once a month (1 out of 20 trips).

Case *Campusbahn* Aachen (Germany), Still no Tram

A positive SCBA is considered to be a primary condition for many projects. However, a positive outcome does not automatically mean that a community will accept the plan. Our case from Aachen, Germany, where project '*Campusbahn*' was cancelled in early 2013, had a score of 1.5, which is considerably higher than the required 1. A vast majority of the inhabitants rejected the plan in a referendum. This plan would have involved the start of a tramway connection of the city centre with the campus in the north-western part of the city (see Chapter 7). Transport demand has increased considerably over the years and the maximum capacity of the bus system on this route has almost been reached.

The similarity with the *Uithof line* case is striking. Like the Uithof, Melaten is a university area and is situated near the edge of the urban agglomeration and is part of a knowledge centre that also includes tertiary education and related businesses. Aachen municipality and the university collaborate on expanding corporate activities, which results in a growing number of students and employees commuting to the campus on a daily basis. Both Utrecht and Aachen aspire to make accessibility sustainable and stimulate the use of bikes and public transport (PT). Aachen distinguishes itself because it strives after 'electrification of the city'. The modality of the tram was preferred, because it is reliable, high-quality and electric. The current bus service just will not do anymore. People complain to the media, so the city and the university are looking for alternatives. The current bus service that connects Aachen city centre with the university faces the very same problems that correspond with the three main effects of unreliability that we have covered in this chapter. For instance, the average travel time is too long, there is a large variation in arrival time, and buses are too crowded. The latter is the main source of complaint.

Terminus Vaals at Dutch border, August 1973. The *Campusbahn* would have mirrored much of this former network that closed in September 1974.

The *Campusbahn* would have complemented the successful *EuregionBahn*, a regional train system serving the city and its cross-border urban region.

6.2 RELIABILITY EFFECTS IN SOCIETAL COST—BENEFIT ANALYSES

As was stated in the Introduction, reliability effects only play a small part in Dutch SCBAs for PT projects. This phenomenon is given more attention in road projects, though research shows that a traditional approach is not project-specific and prone to underestimation. This approach includes reliability effects with a value of 25% of travel time benefits. Though there are similarities between road traffic and PT, calculating reliability benefits in PT is more complex, because it involves a set timetable and travellers and vehicles behave independently. The wait time in particular is a significant aspect. These days it is possible to calculate the effects and translate them into benefits and include them in an SCBA, since more data have become available. We have developed the following plan for this:

1. Calculating vehicle effects, e.g., punctuality and regularity of the system, but also travel time and variation in travel time;
2. Based on step 1 and our new approach (see framed text in Chapter 5) traveller effects are calculated. These are added average travel time and varied travel time. Traveller effects are expressed in additional travel time and a standard deviation of travel time;
3. Using the amounts of money travellers are willing to pay for (reduced) travel time and its variation, things can then be monetized.

This plan distinguishes two important aspects as input for an SCBA. The first is the traveller effect (steps 1 and 2) of a project or development. Its quantity is indicated with 'Q' (Quantity). The second aspect is 'P' (Price; step 3), the value per effect unit. Many studies target P in SCBAs about reliability in PT. Q, the duration of travel time in minutes and the size of standard deviation, used to be given less attention, but can now be calculated using the approach outlined in Chapter 5.

Fig. 6.5 shows the steps of calculation that can be taken to apply the aforementioned in an SCBA. Data on vehicles and travellers are used to

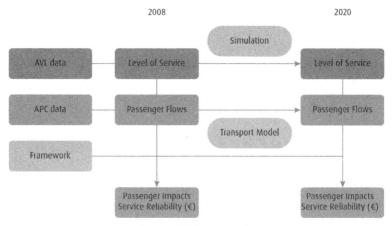

Figure 6.5 Framework.

decide the operation quality and traveller flows, respectively. Our approach can help translate these data into traveller effects of unreliability. To find out what the expected traveller effects are in future situations the same can be done using simulation techniques and traffic models. The difference in effects can be included in an SCBA using values of time and reliability.

Not only is (un)reliability left out of SCBAs, it is also missing from the main tool for PT planning: traffic models. It is still unusual to include PT reliability as a decisive variable in traffic models with the aim of determining the effects of the decision-making process. Further developments in traffic models are required to strengthen the aforementioned approach in SCBAs. We have developed a three-step plan to include PT reliability explicitly in a traffic model in the short term. In addition to theoretic development this approach has also been applied successfully in the traffic model of the Utrecht region. This approach roughly consists of three things: the first is calculating the dynamics of the operations; the second is its translation into traveller effects (both extension of and variation in travel time); and the third is to convert them to travel time using monetary financial ratios for the value of time and the value of reliability. Traffic models can then have their way with travel-time effects, so all functionalities can be used for prognoses.

The development and application of the three-step plan in the Utrecht model is, as far as we know, unique, and illustrates that the method can be used successfully with the desired and latest insights. It is also a stepping stone to more applications, like different regional or national models.

6.3 CASE STUDY *UITHOF LINE* UTRECHT (NETHERLANDS)

Our theoretical framework for (un)reliability effects in SCBAs has been applied to our *Uithof line* case. We here describe the approach and results of the SCBA for the Utrecht *Uithof line*. A light rail line has been planned between Utrecht Central Station and the Uithof and a positive SCBA score is needed to obtain a financial contribution from the Ministry of Infra-structure and the Environment.

The quality of the bus line between Utrecht Central Station and the Uithof was poor at the time of the study. The line has a scheduled travel time of approximately 18 min and transported about 30,000 travellers a day in 2011.

Though this PT line is operated with double-articulated buses at a frequency of 23 times per hour, capacity is limited. On a daily basis travellers tend to be unable to board the first bus they encounter during peak hours and, instead, they have to board the second or third bus. Only a part of the route has its own bus lane and at other parts there are conflicts with pedestrians, cyclists and drivers, resulting in disturbances. Bunching of two or three vehicles is not unusual. The current *Uithof line* is known to be unreliable: the average deviation from schedule per bus is larger than the planned interval, which is about 4 min.

The Uithof is situated in East Utrecht and forms a knowledge cluster that includes tertiary education, the hospital, and related businesses. The municipality is planning to increase corporate activity by approximately 25%. Ultimately, around 53,000 students and 30,000 employees will visit the area on a daily basis. In addition to corporate growth, the municipality also wants to stimulate bicycle and PT transport to achieve sustainable accessibility. There are no plans for extra parking spaces for cars. Traffic prognoses predict a growth up to 45,000 travellers a day on line 12 (the present Uithof bus line) in 2020. At least 50 buses per hour would be needed to meet the required capacity, but the present infrastructure cannot process this amount.

A new, high-quality PT connection has been designed between Utrecht Central Station and the Uithof to cope with the increase in the number of travellers. Light rail was preferred for this, because it offers a reliable and high-quality service. The *Uithof line* will be 8 km long and will have a peak frequency of between 16 and 20 vehicles per hour per direction (Fig. 6.6).

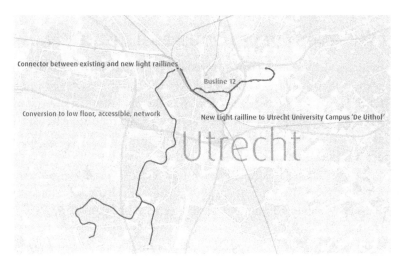

Figure 6.6 Route of new tramway to De Uithof; and old busline and existing tramway.

A big advantage of light rail compared to bus exploitation is, in addition to avoiding direct emissions, that fewer vehicles are needed to meet the transportation demand. This lower intensity enables good traffic flow, because there are fewer conflicts with other road users like drivers and cyclists. Also, the probability of bunching, or the accordion effect, is smaller, which is good for maintaining reliability. In general, investment costs and exploitation costs of light rail are higher than those of a bus, in particular because Utrecht does not yet have an extensive urban rail network. A societal cost—benefit analysis is a good tool to provide insight into the costs and benefits. In addition to this, an SCBA can help optimize alternatives. The alternatives and results of the *Uithof line* SCBA are dealt with in the rest of this chapter.

Prior to the construction of the *Uithof line* the Ministry of Infrastructure and the Environment made €110 million available, provided that the SCBA would have a positive outcome. In other words, the project would have to be cost-effective for society. Though improved reliability was expected to account for a large part of the benefits, it was not yet customary in the Netherlands to make these benefits quantitative. However, scientific research was available and it included a method to calculate reliability from travellers' points of view. This approach, as presented in the previous sections, was thus applied for the first time. Five alternatives to the *Uithof line* were established in cooperation with the regional transit authority (BRU) to come to a fair comparison of all SCBA alternatives. These alternatives ware chosen for their wide range of solutions, analysing on the one hand both bus and light rail, and on the other hand both an existing route and a new route. The five alternatives and different routes are summarized in Table 6.2.

Alternative 1: alternative of reference — This alternative has bus line 12 drive the present route with double-articulated buses and at the current

Table 6.2 Overview of Investigated Alternatives

	Name	Description
1	0-variant (reference 2020)	Bus via current route
2	0 + (2020)	Bus via current route, small adjustments infrastructure
3	BRT Light (2020)	New bus infrastructure, 30 buses/hour/direction
4	BRT (2020)	New bus infrastructure, 50 buses/hour/direction
5	LRT (2020)	New tram infrastructure

frequency of 23 times per hour. Though there is demand for higher transport capacity, introducing a higher frequency is pointless, because travellers will not perceive it as such due to the infrastructure. The result of this will be that travellers will be left behind at stops on a regular basis or have to pass on buses calling. High frequencies combined with high transport demand and interaction with other road users will result in on-route delays, and thus increased (variation in) travel time.

Alternative 2: 0 + alternative — The aim of the 0 + alternative is to offer maximum transport capacity of the bus line on the current route with acceptable reliability. The frequency is enhanced to 25 buses per direction per hour to cope with part of the increase in demand. In order to enable this increased frequency, small adjustments must be made. They may include priority at traffic lights and dedicated PT lanes at crossroads (at the expense of cars). The line 12 travel time (and its variation), hindrance included, will be slightly lower than in alternative 1.

Alternative 3: high-quality bus — This is the first of two newly developed bus alternatives and utilizes the new 'Om de Zuid' route, the present preliminary design of the bus lane. Compared to alternatives 1 and 2 this allows frequency to be increased to 30 buses per direction per hour. The capacity of this bus lane coincides with the PTT (the new Public Transport Terminal at Utrecht Central Station) and stops at the Uithof and is likely to be insufficient to execute the service adequately. Alternative 4 therefore includes additional infrastructural measures.

The Om de Zuid route allows interaction with other road users at same-level crossings, but less frequently than the present route of bus line 12, because the new route avoids busy crossings. However, the increased frequency will cause more obstructions, because there will be more interactions with PT vehicles (both of line 12 and of other lines), especially at the PTT and the Uithof stops.

Alternative 4: high-quality bus+ — This is the second, new bus alternative. The design of the bus lane described in alternative 3 is altered for alternative 4 in such a way that it is capable of meeting the entire transport demand (59 buses per direction per hour). To enable this, extra space to stop has to be created at Utrecht Central Station and the route will be provided with new, different-level crossings (bridges or tunnels) to minimize interactions with other road users. A route parallel to the present bus lane will be created at the Uithof to make sure line 12 and other lines do not affect one another. The reliability of high-quality bus + will be greater than the reliability of the regular high-quality bus of alternative 3.

Alternative 5: *High-quality tram* — The tram route is the same as the route described in the high-quality bus routes. However, the design differs in several points: some of the different-level crossings that are needed in alternative 4 are not needed in alternative 5. The planned frequency will be reduced to 16 trams an hour compared to alternative 4, because trams have larger capacity than buses.

The low floor Urbos 3 CAF LRV during tests at the terminus of the new line at the Uithof (October 14, 2017). The tram is using tracks of the open air depot beyond the tram station. *(Image by Jaap van der Noordt.)*

This SCBA has quantitatively taken reliability effects into account in the aforementioned approach. An analysis has been made of vehicle and traveller data from 2008, as well as a prognosis for 2020. To find out what the traveller effects of unreliable PT are (and, therefore, the effects of improvements) we used vehicle data of the current situation. Using the regional traffic model (VRU model) we made prognoses of the transport demand of the different alternatives and we also calculated future vehicle and transport data, using simulations. To do this, we had to estimate divisions in processes like stopping and driving for the new situations to determine the traveller effects of unreliability.

Table 6.3 shows the expected reliability effects for each alternative. The calculation is based on an analysis of current reliability, specifically average extra in-vehicle time per traveller (compared to the timetable) and its variation. What is also included is the average extra wait time caused by

Table 6.3 Overview of Characteristics of Alternatives

	Alt. 1	Alt. 2	Alt. 3	Alt. 4	Alt. 5
Frequency morning peak (/hour/direction)	23×	25×	30×	59×	16×
Trip time, one direction (timetable)	22 min	21 min	19 min	17 min	17 min
Average waiting time (timetable)	1.3 min	1.2 min	1 min	0.5min	1.9 min
Additional in-vehicle time	2 min	2 min	2 min.	0.6 min	0 min
Distribution, additional in-vehicle time (σ)	2 min	1.7 min	1.5 min	0.6 min	0 min
Additional waiting time	2.9 min	2 min	1.0 min	0 min	0 min
Distribution, additional waiting time (σ)	1.4 min	1 min	0.5 min	0 min	0 min
Average travel time, Central Station—Uithof (including waiting)	28 min	26 min	23 min	18 min	19 min

unreliability per traveller and its variation. The average travel time (which comprises waiting and moving) between Utrecht Central Station and the Uithof has also been indicated. As a consequence of several variables, some travellers will be confronted with longer travel times and others with shorter travel times.

It can be concluded that the wait time is shortest in alternative 4 because of the high frequency and that unreliability is relatively low, so the extra travel time and variation in travel time are high. Alternatives 4 and 5 are expected to have high reliability and therefore to be low in extra travel time and variation in travel time. The large number of buses in alternative 4 increases the chance of disruptions compared to alternative 5. There will be variation in alternative 5 service operation, which can never be prevented entirely, but the effects on travellers will be minimal.

After the traveller effects had been determined, they were monetized using values of time and reliability that were available at the time. Table 6.4 shows the costs and benefits for each aspect, including the overall score. The results from previous sections are an important input for this. Results are shown in the net present value (NPV) and the cost—benefit rate. It is shown that the reliability benefits are substantial for all alternatives and the ratio would be considerably lower without these rates. Alternatives 3, 4 and 5 would score even less than 1, which would not render them cost-effective for society.

Table 6.4 Overview of Costs and Benefits per Alternative, Including Cost-Benefit Ratio (With and Without Consideration of Service Reliability Impacts)

	Net Value in Millions of Euros			
Alternatives	2	3	4	5
Effects				
Investment costs	−1	−93	−237	−222
Operational costs	2	−6	−33	−66
Travel time gains	30	52	89	67
Service Reliability				
Decreased additional travel time	20	39	100	123
Decreased distribution travel time	20	36	60	78
Increased probability finding a seat	0	0	2	4
Latent demand	0	0	6	5
Jobs	4	8	16	18
Emissions	0	+	−	+
Noise	0	0	−1	1
Traffic safety	0	0	−2	1
Hindrance to other traffic	0	−1	3	1
Hinder During Construction				
Car	0	−	−	−
PT	0	−	− −	−
Future proof	−	−	+	++
Societal acceptance	− −	−	− −	+
Total costs	2	−99	−270	−288
Total benefits	80	158	311	336
Benefits minus costs	81	59	40	8
Benefit/costs ratio	**++**	**1.6**	**1.1**	**1.2**
Benefit/costs ratio without service reliability benefits	*++*	*0.8*	*0.6*	*0.5*

What is also shown, is that investment costs are high in both alternatives 4 and 5, but they do have high reliability benefits. These are approximately two-thirds of the total benefits. The alternative preferred by the region, alternative 5 (light rail), turns out to be societally cost-efficient; with the ratio greater than 1.

Reliability is an important aspect of quality of PT, for both travellers and operators. Many PT projects, especially the light rail-related ones, therefore target its improvement. The decision-making process tends to be aided by SCBAs that include PT reliability quantitatively. Based on the *Uithof line* case we can conclude that the approach we envisioned can be applied in practice and that the reliability benefits are substantial and can even be crucial for the cost—benefit ratio. We expect this to apply to more light-rail projects. We therefore advise the approach presented here to be included in the formal SCBA standards (e.g., Dutch guidelines like 'OEI-leidraad'). Either a detailed or a quick-scan approach can be chosen, based on the project and the effects expected. Decision-making support will be improved when these benefits are included quantitatively, rather than left out.

Our approach is mainly concerned with travellers and it is important to make traveller effects known. However, reliability indicators and plans for improvement often target supply, that is, vehicles. Well-known factors are punctuality and regularity of trams and buses.

Our approach roughly comprises three steps. The first step is to determine variation on the supply side. The second step is to transfer these effects by means of a mathematical framework to traveller effects, which are extra travel time per traveller and its variation. The third step is to monetize these effects using values of time and reliability, after which they are ready to be used as input for the SCBA. This approach helped us show that reliability benefits make up for two-thirds of the total expected benefits for the *Uithof line* project. The high-quality alternatives would not have had a positive SCBA score if these benefits had not been formulated explicitly.

Not only reliability, but also comfort benefits are included too infrequently in cost—benefit analyses. This also plays an important part in light rail. Research is currently being conducted at Delft University of Technology to take this aspect more explicitly into account, so that better assessments can be made.

CHAPTER 7

Making Light Rail

Our account of light rail (and other forms of high-quality public transport) is based on many cases and examples. Our two Dutch cases of *RandstadRail* and *Uithof line* have been covered extensively in the Chapters 5 and 6. This chapter deals with more cases to track factors of failure and lessons for success. The Groningen case, our third Dutch main case in this regard, will be covered in detail.

7.1 OVERVIEW OF INCREMENTAL PLANNING

Though there are plenty of arguments and advantages to light rail, swift planning and construction of light rail are not very commonly mentioned. Urban planning projects are always complex, especially when infrastructure is included. This is illustrated in Peter Hall's classic study — the title of his book *Great Planning Disasters* says it all. Many large projects are doomed to fail. They cause unexpectedly high costs and often have defects, if they are realized at all. Unfortunately, many tram projects fall under this category in the sense that they are constructed slowly and with a lot of complications. Even if a tramway is eventually operated successfully, often the preceding planning process has undergone extreme difficulties.

A classic example of such a project is the introduction of the new Dublin tram *Luas*, which is 'speed' in Irish. Irish Times journalist Frank McDonald covered the history of large urban planning and infrastructural works (like the redevelopment of the Docklands and the Dublin Port Tunnel) in the Irish capital during the economic boom of the 1990s in his book *The Construction of Dublin*. McDonald describes the planning history of *Luas* from 1987 to 2000 very precisely. It is a dramatic history fuelled by considerable prejudice. The local Dublin government faced constant opposition from within and without. The decision to start construction was made after years of struggles, but this resulted in great delays, because it was then proposed to have parts of the tram go underground, which would result in considerably higher costs and new rounds of public and political debate.

Light Rail Transit Systems
ISBN 978-0-12-814784-9
https://doi.org/10.1016/B978-0-12-814784-9.00007-4

The tram system finally opened in 2004. It encompassed two lines that are, unfortunately, not connected in the centre because of the fruitless tunnel discussions. Extensions were constructed in the years after. *Line A* crosses the entire city from west to east, right up the new working and living area of the Docklands. *Line B* will not be extended through the centre in a northern direction until late 2017, crossing *Line A* overground. By that time it will have taken 30 years to get the tram completely up and running. The *Luas* tram system is now an essential part of Dublin. Its importance and success are obvious, because the tram transports more passengers than it had ever been intended to do. Also, its operation is cost-covering; there is no government subsidy.

The new light rail system of Dublin is called 'Luas', which means 'speed' in Irish.

The *Luas* project is certainly not exceptional. Our list of projects that do not run smoothly is easily expanded, such as with the Edinburgh tram, whose construction problems have been dealt with in the media on a regular basis. In the end the intended project was curtailed and the line from the airport to the city centre opened in 2014. We studied this project specifically concerning its contract form (see later in this chapter).

Our case on the tram project in Jerusalem turned out to be even more difficult. Based on field work and interviews on the spot we were able to conclude that the main cause of the long delay was the deficient project organization. The controversial status of the project — the tramway crosses the border between Israel and the West Bank — also prevented efficient planning. The line became operative step by step from late 2011, but during the first years it faced many problems related to the social segregation in Jerusalem.

Our second case from Israel, the light rail project in Tel Aviv, went even worse. The first version of the project failed. The contract form studied by us may have played a part in that, because the tender failed in 2009. The project was given a second chance in a changed form in 2011. The same thing happened with the *Spårväg City* project in Stockholm; an amateurish organization and the complexity of the contract caused the project to fail. Unlike Tel Aviv, the restart, this time with a conventional organization and tender, was successful and the first phase opened in 2010. The tramway has been extended and will be connected to existing tramways in the urban Stockholm region (more about this case further on in this chapter about contract forms).

After having considered these examples the only conclusion that can be drawn is that exceeding costs are the rule, not the exception. Costs related to construction and organizational and institutional complexity mainly seem to be underestimated. Danish researcher Bent Flyvbjerg concludes in his studies that many rail projects face considerable cost overruns and less use is made of the project than had been expected before the opening. This is not the place to cover Flyvbjerg's conclusions extensively, let alone refute them. We would like to make some remarks on his definition of projects. 'Rail', and even 'urban rail', are very general terms, which makes it impossible to make a distinction between, for example, complex and expensive metro projects and more pragmatic and cost-efficient light rail projects. Moreover, from the cases we researched it generally turns out that the ridership of new tramways is considerably larger than had been projected. Also, Flyvbjerg does not put enough consideration into the difference between European and American projects. This could explain the disappointing ridership he mentions. In many case implemented ridership figures in the US are to low according European standards. Finally, tram projects are especially long projects in changing contexts in terms of government and city. This makes it difficult to consider them as one project and research them as such.

Paris T1, terminus in the northern banlieues.

Our case of the *T1* tram project in Paris seems to confirm Flyvbjerg's statements when it comes to cost overruns, though the scope of transport is much larger than expected. Besides, a tram project like this is about more than just transport, which justifies questions about a singular interpretation of high construction costs. Based on research from the early 1990s it can be concluded that the civic significance of this project is considerable. From the first stage (the line from Saint-Denis via La Corneuve to Bobigny, which opened in 1992) onwards it had been clear that this project was going to be so much more than just an improvement in transport. The tram was explicitly meant to improve the planning and social structures of the neighbourhoods it served. The face of the city changed along the entire line as a result of the way the tram project transformed the public space.

The project has been studied since the early 1980s and arguments in favour of a tram were frequently made. The ambitious task, an indecisive national government, and three bordering municipalities that had a say in things delayed the project so much that construction could not begin until 1990. When the tramway opened 2 years later it turned out that the cost had been higher than expected and on top of all that, just 10 years after the opening a large part of the infrastructure had to be completely renovated. Being a pioneer has caused the *T1* project many problems. In spite of that, subsequent tram projects in Paris, including several extensions to *T1*, have turned out to be more expensive than expected.

The tram-train project on the island of La Réunion (France DROM). The LRVs should have run almost entirely along the coast.

Though the success of the tram in France is well known it does not mean that all projects can be implemented without any problems; especially tram-train projects are subject to delays, or even cancellations. A very special example is the ambitious project for a new, regional tramway in the French overseas department of La Réunion. It could be concluded from our research on the spot that the project was going to be an institutionally complex, very expensive, and very ambitious tram-train project. A pragmatic approach and, therefore, a smaller scope of the project was not acceptable, not even when it turned out that the available money from Paris was not going to be sufficient. After the reigning communist party had dramatically lost elections, the project was soon cancelled. The new government replaced the intended express tram with a motorway and bus project in 2010. The completed tender was ignored and the selected consortium, which was going to build and operate the line, left empty handed.

Without meaning to, this set the example of ignoring a tender in Groningen in a similar way 3 years later, but before we get to Groningen, there are two other tram-train projects we would like to discuss. A tram-train project in the urban region of Stavanger-Sandnes in Norway had been under preparation for years. The trams were supposed to run from the city into the region and several sections of the proposed line would include track sharing with heavy rail trains from the national operator. This plan was so technically and administratively difficult that traditional solutions using trams or buses became more appealing. It turned out from our on-site experience with this case that the initial idea of a tram-train solution made this project unnecessarily complicated, resulting in the fact that even the possibility of a tram was not an actual option since 2012.

In spite of the complexity tram-train projects are associated with, it seemed a pragmatic and feasible approach for the urban region of Léon in Spain. The idea was to run a diesel-electric tram service on adjusted railway tracks and to combine this with a short route for a city tram in Léon itself. Construction works for adjusting the main tracks had already started and the hybrid LRVs and city trams were ready in the Vossloh España factory when the project was stopped in 2012 as a result of unexpectedly severe cutbacks.

A tram-train project that was realized in the German state of Saarland has to be included in this overview. Our *Saarbahn* case had been equipped with the latest tram-train technologies (from Bombardier) and it functioned as an example for *RandstadRail* in the Netherlands because of its function as the designated stimulant of transport and economy in the urban region of Saarbrücken. Designing and planning the first phase of the line could start when, after difficult debates, it had been decided that the line should pass by the city centre, instead of going straight through it. The first phase of the project was concluded in 1997 when the line between Saarbrücken and Sarreguemines, just across the border with France, was opened. However, the extension to Lebach, which had been intended from the onset, was not constructed until 2014, after a 15-year delay. The remaining plans to serve other towns in Saarland were not finalized, even though the national government had generously subsidized the project to encourage the Saarland economy. A number of institutional obstacles, like the administrative independence (or wilfulness) of several municipalities, prevented further extensions. The intended shared use of German and French main lines eliminated the original plan. The institutional complexity of tram projects may be large, but the complexities of tram-train projects are virtually impossible to overcome. The history of the *RandstadRail* case has taught us this much, but the same conclusion can be drawn from elaborate European research, conducted by German tram-train expert Axel Kuehn, into these kinds of project. His research shows that tram-train projects are neither cheap, nor easy to realize.

The problems tend to be so big that the tram project is ended prematurely. Some of these projects are revived years later in a changed or even completely different form. The Luxembourg tram-train project is an example of this. It was intended in 2003 to become a regional network around the capital, but was stopped less than 10 years later. In spite of this there will be a tram in Luxembourg City. The current project will provide an urban tramway that will be opened in stages from 2017 to 2021.

The way things went in Kiel, Germany, was the other way around. There used to be an operational city tramway there and it was the busiest corridor of the public transport network. However, in 1985, the year when the first of the new-generation tram systems opened in Nantes, France, it was decided to shut down the tramway in Kiel. More than 20 years later the *StadtRegionalBahn*, a tram-train system for the Kiel urban region, was introduced. A demonstration of the *RegioCitadis* from Kassel was held on the railway between Kiel and Neumünster in 2007 but still planning was halted in 2013, mainly because bordering municipalities proved uncooperative. In this way Kiel proves to be yet another example of how complex government structures in urban regions can be disastrous for tram-train plans. The same thing happened in our RijnGouwelijn case. Kiel is not the only German city where reintroduction of the tram failed. Hamburg and Aachen (Aix-La-Chapelle) have tried the same thing twice each. There have been plans in Hamburg for years to change one of the busiest bus lines into a tramway. Solid arguments have been raised for this, like reliability and comfort for travellers and lower costs for the operator. Twice advanced plans ready for construction have been turned down, once by a Christian democratic and once by a social democratic government. The plan to create an express tram between Bramfeld and Altona will not be realized any time soon.

Our case from Aachen (Germany) will be covered next. After the first project for a *Stadtbahn* was shut down in 1999 because of presumed high costs, the *Campusbahn*, which was going to be the second tram project in this city, was cancelled in early 2013. A referendum was held and a large majority of the inhabitants voted against the plan that entailed the first phase of a tramway that was to connect the city centre with the university neighbourhood in the northwest of the city. It is questionable whether all arguments were seriously considered in this referendum. Transport demand had increased significantly over the years and the maximum capacity of the bus system on this route had been reached. Besides, the chamber of commerce had pointed out the economic importance of a tram. Finally, the tram would have entailed the transition to electric transport. There are some indications of bad communication in respect to this project, which seems to be confirmed by research conducted by 'RWTH Aachen', who, like the university, are advocates of the arrival of a tram.

Our other relevant cases here are those from England. They involved projects in which many investments were made, but which were shut down anyway. They include the light rail projects of Bristol (2004 †), Leeds (2004 †), Liverpool (2005–08 †), and Portsmouth (2004–06 †). Every project had different reasons for its demise. Irreconcilable differences of opinion between the city board and the boards of the surrounding rural towns prevented the Bristol 'supertram' from ever being realized, while an expensive tram tunnel was considered necessary for the *South Hampshire Rapid Transit* project in Portsmouth. What these failed planning processes have in common, is that local governments depend on the central government for financially contributing to the project. This dependence caused the English projects to be insufficiently financially disciplined at a local level, even more so than for their continental counterparts. The Department for Transport (DfT) withdrew its initial financial commitment for the Liverpool *Merseytram* and the Leeds *Supertram* after the costs had gone up considerably. The national government lacked involvement in these projects. DfT refused to reconsider its negative decision in the Portsmouth case, though the public benefits and yields were demonstrably high. The same applied for the Liverpool Merseytram; a well-argued restart was boycotted without any reasons being provided. It was finally and definitely refused in 2008. The city of Liverpool made some fruitless attempts to revive the projects in the years after, for example using completely private financing.

Finally there is London, where three tram projects can be reported. One of these is the Croydon project, but this is not included in our overview of projects that faced difficult planning (the case is included in the section on tendering and contracting later in this chapter). The other two projects are the *Cross River Tram*, in the centre of the city between Camden and King's Cross, and the *Uxbridge tram* (*West London Tram*) to Sheperd's Bush in the west of the city. Then-mayor Ken Livingston was in charge of both projects. The latter project never got beyond the initial stages and was postponed indefinitely in 2008 because it was opposed by the councils of the Boroughs involved. The former project was shut down by the then-new mayor Boris Johnson in the same year.

All of this raises the question why English tram projects are so much more expensive than elsewhere in Europe. There are at least three reasons for this. Legal expenditures are always very high because of British laws and regulations and the subsequent way social risks are dealt with in the UK. Then there are indications that complementary entries take up a large part of the budget. This mainly goes for replacing often very old underground infrastructure of cables and mains. The third reason is the absence of urban—regional government in the UK, which damages nearly all plans. Though London has a metropolitan mayor it is still a combination of a number of autonomous boroughs. Our Manchester case of the light rail system *Metrolink*, which opened in 1992, is an exception as a regional transport authority. Manchester is England's first new tram city and not without good reason; its network has been extended more than any other.

It is remarkable that hardly any progress has been made in coming up with alternative plans for high-quality public transport nearly 10 years later. The plans for a guided bus in Bristol have come to nothing, while improvement of the regional train network only goes very slowly. Leeds has made some progress planning a trolleybus network but cancelled this project too. High-quality bus alternatives apparently face the same civic barriers as tram projects. A possible light rail system in the Bristol urban region has been worked on more recently.

Many experiences with the previous cases, the English ones in particular, have been shared and applied in advice projects and research projects, like the Intereg project HiTrans (2002—05) about the development of high-quality public transport for medium-sized cities and their regions, as well as the research into potential benefits and barriers to public transport in metropoles and urban regions by Next Generation Infrastructures (NGInfra, 2010—12). Some cases have recently been used to define the characteristics of light rail for the European Metropolitan Transport

Authorities (Van der Bijl and Van Oort, 2014). The Dutch projects of *RandstadRail* and *Uithof line*, which were covered in previous chapters, have been taken into account here.

Vélez-Málaga and Jaén (Spain)

It is well known that projects can be shut down in the planning phase and that a lot of things can go wrong during the construction stage, but a light rail project being shut down at the time of operation does not happen very often. This is why two Spanish cities deserve a special place in our collection of problematic projects. A new tramway opened in Vélez-Málaga in 2006, but was shut down 6 years later in 2012. The tram project in Jaén was even more remarkable: a new tramways operated for only two weeks in May 2011. Vélez-Málaga had over-estimated transport demand, which turned out to be much lower than antici-pated. The municipality lacked the money to compensate the operator.

Impressions from the work in Vélez-Málaga during October 2005, a year before opening of the unfortunate tramway.

Vélez-Málaga and Jaén (Spain)—cont'd

The tramway in the city of Jaén will remain closed for the foreseeable future. The municipality does not want to compensate a complaining bus operator for the expected decline in bus transport caused by the arrival of the tram. No one knows if the line will ever be opened, but it is typical for the financial organization of many urban (tram) projects in Spain.

CityPass, the Tram Project of Jerusalem (Israel)

Jaffastreet in the centre of Jerusalem, during the latest stage of construction (November 2010).

Many Israeli projects are internationally deemed controversial and this goes for the *CityPass*, too. Looking at the constructed infrastructure on the route, the tram project does not seem too dissimilar to projects in many European countries. Not surprisingly, its setup is like that of an average tram project in a French city. Running through the centre of the city, the line connects the southwestern part of Jerusalem to the new neighbourhoods in the northeast of the metropolitan area (Pisgat Ze'ev). On the way several important public transport hubs are served, like the central bus station and the future station for high-speed trains to Tel Aviv. Improvement of public space along the route is part of the project. Even a landmark in the form of a spectacular cable-stayed bridge for trams and pedestrians, designed by the renowned architect Calatrava, has been scheduled for construction in the heart of the city.

The main goal of the new tramway (known as the *Red Line*) is to provide a fast connection between Pisgat Ze'ev and the city centre. The fact that Pisgat

Continued

CityPass, the Tram Project of Jerusalem (Israel)—cont'd

Ze'ev and Neve Yaakov, just north of it, are internationally considered settlements instead of neighbourhoods is what makes this tramway controversial, because they are situated on the occupied West Bank. The tram infrastructure fixates this situation. In terms of urban planning this example shows the power of a tramway as an instrument of urban planning. It shows the international community how seriously Israel takes the expansion of its territory on the West Bank.

Planning *CityPass* has been very difficult. Many reasons are thought to be responsible, such as Israel's lack of experience with this kind of infrastructure; the tender of a similar tram project even failed altogether and a divided organization caused several parties to get into legal fights. French transport operator Veolia, which was initially supposed to operate the tram, has doubts concerning whether the infrastructural integration will allow for the time-table settled on. Veolia was under huge international pressure for formally co-operating on an illegal project, which is why the Dutch ASN bank severed all ties with Veolia in 2006. Still, the tram became operational in 2011. The project had progressed too far and was logistically too important for the expanding Israeli part of Jerusalem.

Meanwhile, expansion plans have been elaborated. Most likely Jerusalem will get a network of tramways (and busways) in the near future.

7.2 CASE STUDY *REGIOTRAM* GRONINGEN (NETHERLANDS)

Groningen, a university city in the north-east of the Netherlands, in co-production with the province of the same name, has seriously considered a tramway project, called *Regio Tram* (2008—12). The first stage of this ambitious project entailed two urban lines for opening in 2016 (11.7 km), including improvement of the adjacent public realm. The second stage aimed to realize regional through services on existing heavy real tracks into the region. This track-sharing operation explains the name of the project, *Regio Tram*, and was due to be in service not earlier than 2020.

The main project (i.e., stage 1) comprised an investment of 300 million euros and a Design, Build, Finance, Maintain, Operate contract (including the acquisition of light rail vehicles). Tendering was planned for the period December 2010—12, and construction for 2013—15. The project was assigned by the City of Groningen and the Province of Groningen, in co-operation with regional municipal partners. An independent project office was in charge of content and management. Its project director was directly accountable to an administrative board of executives of the city and province. Funding of Line 1 was agreed between the city, province and their partners; a package deal with the national government guaranteed the funding of Line 2. In December 2010 three consortia were selected to deliver their proposals for the project 2 years later (December 2012).

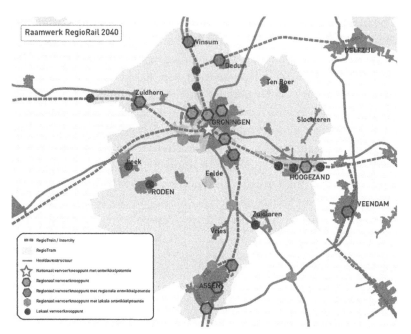

Maps of the proposed networks for the city and region, respectively.

For years the city of Groningen (190,000 inhabitants) and its surrounding area (inner and greater regions; 600,000 and 1.5 million inhabitants, respectively) had been working on this tram project, exploring the options for a tram in Groningen well before the official start of the project in 2008. The exploration of ideas (1995−2001) and the first serious planning studies (2001−07) had preceded the opening of the *RegioTram* project organization (2008). However, the city council shut this project down, just before the planning process and tender would have been successfully concluded, as there was a good offer from at least one market party, much to the astonishment of the province and other regional governments.

A contemporary cartoon featured a green *RegioTram* (green was going to be the colour of the vehicles) that was driven off the tracks by a red van of the local social democratic party (PvdA). The image is similar to the way the party was portrayed in the media; it was depicted as a Stalinist organization that had forced its will upon the Groningen council for years.

However, it was not the social democrats who helped eliminate the *RegioTram* project, but the aldermen of the local liberal (D66) and socialist (SP) parties. The Groningen Socialist Party especialy, had always been critical of the project because they claimed it would be financially reckless. But was it really financially reckless?

The first explorations were conducted around 1995. Things started going faster 10 years later when a delegation from Groningen visited the French city of Valenciennes where a similar project had been completed successfully (see A Visit to Valenciennes (France) box). By that time it was clear that the local public transport system in Groningen had to be adjusted to the increasing traffic. A project organization that the province and municipality were responsible for was founded in 2007. Then-alderman Ms Karin Dekker, an ambitious *GroenLinks* (Green Party) politician, was to be its representative. The project organization was given the assignment to earnestly investigate the option of a tram. Initially one tramway line was intended to be constructed and it was supposed to run from the city centre to the university's Zernike Campus on the northern outskirts of the city. However, a second line (to the neighbourhood of Kardinge in the northeast) was added when the new project organization was given the task of realizing a new tram project within the available budget. A new form of tender was expected. This form was a DBFMO and it comprised a long-term consortium that provides Design, Building, partial Financing, Maintenance, and Operation, including purchase and maintenance of the tram vehicles (see our research into such tender forms later in this chapter). Besides staying on budget, the operation had to be cost neutral compared to the existing bus transport and the business case over the 25.5 years of the DBFMO contract had to be financially conclusive. Also, all output specifications had to be met. Finally, the offer of the market parties should not exceed a specified maximum.

All these demands were granted late in 2012. Though the tender had not been formally concluded, at least one of the two offering market parties had placed a valid offer. Still, the project failed. Every democratic government body has 'the right to make bad decisions', responsible Provincial-Executive (*Gedeputeerde* in Dutch) William Moorlag (province of Groningen) concluded afterwards.

The narrow street in the historic centre (Oosterstraat) was the focus of the negative issues. The tram was not considered to be a solution for the bus problem.

The *RegioTram* project had been prepared in all earnestness, but failed nonetheless. It would be easy to blame the two previously mentioned aldermen, but the planning process was too difficult for that. Several causes can be found with hindsight. In the first place, there was not enough public support from residents and stakeholders. The history of Groningen has to be kept in mind in order to understand this; the last passenger tramway there was shut down in 1949 and the older residents' memories of it were not exactly positive. The supposed disadvantages of the tram (old-fashioned, too large, dangerous) influenced public perspective on this line, especially in the city centre. This view mainly applied to the Oosterstraat, a narrow shopping street in the city centre where a great number of buses run in one direction. The plan for a tram replaced these buses with trams in both directions. Residents and shopkeepers feared hindrance and problems with delivery of supplies. An alternative featuring a single track was proposed after reconsideration. This was to be the solution to a complicated puzzle. However, resistance remained, which is understandable considering the Oosterstraat was not even going to get its own tram stop. This decision was understandable from the operational point of view, but the symbolic value of such a stop would have increased public support.

Artist impression of a proposed alignment at the city centre.

Integrating the project in the Grote Markt ('Great Market', the main square in the historic city centre) may have been a controversial task, because the tram project would coincide there with a large urban project. The Grote Markt would become smaller and on the back side of it the new Forum, providing public cultural facilities, would be built. The decision makers involved saw things going downhill.

This sums up the dilemma; on the one hand the route through Groningen city centre was both cause and justification of the project, but on the other hand the same route was an unacceptable option for many.

A second important cause for the failure of the project was the so-called 'extension of scope' during the planning process. A second line was added to the original line to the Zernike Campus, after preparations had already been made for the latter. This prolonged the planning process by at least a year. New procedures had to be started and the new line fuelled new discussions with residents, other stakeholders, and services of the municipality of Groningen.

'Tram No Way' in many display windows marked the protests against the tram project.

The third reason was the choice to combine the tender with a complex and innovative contract form (DBFMO). Never before had a tramway project in the Netherlands had a contract form like this and even in other countries it was a rarity. Besides, a DBFMO procedure takes up more time for several reasons. Also, a DBFMO procedure makes communication with the outside world difficult once the tender process has been started; all information between the organization of the project and market parties is confidential.

Faltering communication was the fourth reason for the demise of the *RegioTram* project. The project used to be viewed positively in spite of the Oosterstraat objections. Communication was arranged well within the organization. In mid-2007 the project was given a lot of attention during an event in the city centre, but during the tender phase (2010–12) it got a lot quieter. The civil servants responsible did not draw too much attention to the project for 'tactical reasons' and neither did the office responsible for the realization of the tramway. At the same time opponents made themselves heard, primarily via social media, especially Twitter. Residents' and shopkeepers' participation was now frowned upon and public support was shattered. People were dissatisfied with the tram and pamphlets saying 'Tram No Way' were put up in shop windows.

Three major issues shut down the project for good. First and foremost there was the changing political context. After the 2010 elections for the municipal council local liberals and socialists (the D66 and SP parties) entered the board of mayor and aldermen (Dutch: *college van burgemeester en wethouders*). The two aldermen responsible for the tram project, Karin Dekker of the Green Party and her social democrat (PvdA) colleague, had to collaborate with parties who were not so positive about the tram. Ms Dekker did not manage to convey the benefits of DBFMO and the notion that the tram was only an expensive toy was able to take root.

The second issue concerned framing the tram project. The project was constantly portrayed as a transport project. The tram had to be implemented to solve a traffic problem; bus capacity was insufficient to cope with the traveller flow to the university campus. During the project emphasis was put on the importance of adequate public space and the benefits of less bus traffic in the historic city centre, but even in this respect the tone of the discussion soon turned negative. Instead of being seen as an opportunity to improve public space, the tram was marked by opponents as an intruder causing damage in the form of noise, vibration and the loss of green space (while the tram project actually involved more of the latter). The tram was seen as a problem and not as a challenge. This sums up the second issue rather well and makes it clear that our elaborate argumentation, as laid out in Chapters 4–6, did not play any significant part in the *RegioTram* project. The effectiveness of light rail was reduced to mere problem solving, while spatially efficient improvement of the city was not sufficiently taken into account. The values of the tramway for public matters like the economy, environment and social inclusion were not visualized. The office responsible even thought that emphasizing these aspects would make the whole thing implausible and the restrictions of the intended DBMFO contract did not exactly help; many of the arguments mentioned in favour are very difficult to quantify immediately.

The third reason why the tram project was never brought into being is, in hindsight, the main one: we think the project suffered from a too technocratic approach. Not only did the choice for a complicated DBFMO contract turn out to be wrong, but also the professional and well-meant attitude of thoroughly getting to the bottom of everything, as well as weighing in all aspects and specifying them technically. A new tramway through the city centre certainly is a matter of civil engineering, but it is also urban planning and a social enterprise. Technical requirements are not always clear, not in the least part because of the large number of parties involved; pros and cons must be weighed. It is important to make clear what the user wishes and what the functional demands are, and to conceptualize the intended solution before proceeding to technical specifications (engineering). The focus is on design; not just on its aesthetic qualities (as is sometimes thought), but also the creation of an unmistakable collection of specifications that caters to all functional demands. Design precedes engineering. Planning urban infrastructure is a difficult task, because projects and financing are often dominated by matters of civil engineering. The temptation or pressure to prioritize engineering is considerable. This is what happened to the Groningen project and it has definitely put pressure on the relationship between the tram project and the municipal urban planning service (ROEZ).

The importance of technical specifications during the design stage was a direct consequence of opting for a DBFMO tender, which requires all financial and other risks to be meticulously assessed quantitatively. It should be noted that a great (theoretic) benefit of the DBFMO tender was also the cause of the failure. Unlike regular tenders, DBFMO tenders require explicitly stating all costs and risks, which reveals both the construction costs and the costs of the 22.5-year operation. The consortium of builder and operator commits to the project from the moment the contract is signed, which provides transparency to the public for a quarter of a century (3 years of construction and 22.5 years of operation).

The benefit of this approach is clear: the government bodies involved will not be confronted with financial blows and politicians know what to expect. At the same time this is a disadvantage, because the costs of the project can function as ammunition for political opponents. This black-box quality of DBFMO and the legal complexity that goes with it caused the downfall of *RegioTram*. Explanation to people involved (civil servants, municipal councillors, residents, and executives) of how DBFMO worked and how the tender could be financially beneficial could not be managed.

Another curious reason for the downfall that needs to be noted is the role of civil servants and (former) executives. Their opposition was a public secret in the municipality of Groningen. Moreover, many former executives did very little to hide their opinions on the project during its final months. When alderman Ms Dekker left her position, former mayor and 'local hero' Jacques Wallage suggested that the tram project would not have gotten out of hand under his supervision, thus pointing out the weaknesses of his successor, who had not taken any action when the project started going amiss. All of this resulted in a longer planning process and a decline in political and public support, which was exactly what opponents needed at the very last moment. In the summer of 2012 the annual municipal budget meetings began. Two critical aldermen from the D66 and SP parties demanded the tram no longer be included in the budget. The municipality's tight financial situation was an understandable argument for this; ever since the start of the financial crisis (4 years earlier, in 2008) many municipalities were financially harmed by the decrease in land value.

Groningen had been especially susceptible to this, since the ambitious new neighbourhood in the east of the city (Meerstad) alone was a huge financial burden. However, around the same time tens of millions of euros were spent on the Forum project and a local bridge (Sontbrug) for a connection with the planned new neighbourhood, whose construction had been delayed because of the financial crisis.

In 2012 the maximum price of the Groningen tram had been set at 452 million euros: more than 300 million for building and planning and the rest was to go on operation. These amounts are realistic according to international standards and the organization of the project succeeded in constructing a feasible plan of reference. All government bodies involved had committed to the maximum price, so the project was financially covered and financing was almost completed. An agreement was finally made about the contribution to the operation costs after the system would have opened. Moreover, the European Investment Bank had promised to contribute.

The project seemed to be sufficiently financially covered. Nonetheless, in 2012 the D66 and SP aldermen announced at their own initiative that they would not support the next year's budget if it still included a tram. This executive coupe forced 'tram aldermen' Karin Dekker (GroenLinks) and her PvdA colleague to surrender their portfolios. Still, the project would not have been lost if the new municipal board, assembled after a rough formation, had been willing to finish the tender or put it on a temporary hold, but the political will was no longer there.

The worries were not unfounded, but it was reckless to stop the project for purely financial reasons; 40 million euros of planning expenses would go down the drain just like that. Moreover, the tram project had included regular urban planning investments, so damages were estimated at at least 80 million euros. The municipality risked losing 115 million euros of money that the national government had put in a compensation fund, which had been created some years before to compensate the north of the Netherlands when a planned high-speed train from Amsterdam to Groningen was cancelled. However, what stands out most is the bizarre timing of it all. The mere fact that the project was shut down just days before the consortia were going to make their final offers, gives rise to the suspicion that political opponents wanted to shut down the project once and for all. Though this may be politically legitimate, efficient and well-balanced governing is not benefited by the continuation of a project at high expenses when the intent had been to sabotage it all along.

In early 2013, Van der Bijl (one of the authors of this book) and engineering company Movares were commissioned by a Provincial Executive of the province of Groningen to research the options of salvaging the project after all. The plan that was researched was one involving the original second phase (extending the line into the area around Groningen) as the new, first phase of the revived project. This was not some randomly chosen notion, since inspiration could be drawn from existing regional light rail projects in, for example, Switzerland and several tram-train projects in France. Our Léon case in Spain also served as an example. Even though the project had been shut down not long before, the idea of starting the project from the surrounding region was inspiring nonetheless. It was advised to investigate how a new tram-train pilot could be initiated on the rail tracks between Groningen and Zuidhorn as a first phase. At the same time the tender for the local train transport should be 'tram-proof' by 2020, as should all new bus infrastructure in the city. Unfortunately, the Provincial Executives could not agree on reintroduction of the tram project, which finalized its demise for good. This is indeed final, because the two tender submissions cannot be used anymore. Legally this information can only be accessed by parties involved in the restricted, but prematurely concluded, DBFMO contract formation.

A Visit to Valenciennes (France)

The tram in Valenciennes contributed to the liveability of this former industrial city.

A Visit to Valenciennes (France)—cont'd

In November 2006 a delegation from Groningen (the Netherlands) went on a study trip to Valenciennes (France). This trip sped up decision-making processes at the time. The similarities with this northern French town unexpectedly and quickly showed what a tram could mean for Groningen. Some months later it was decided to seriously investigate the possibilities of a tram project in Groningen and to found a separate project organization.

After a construction period of more than 2 years, the first phase of the new Valenciennes tram opened on 16 June, 2006. Planning had taken over 13 years to complete; deciding on the route through the city centre especially took up a lot of time. Inhabitants soon became very fond of their tram, which has brought new life to the poor, former coal city.

The first phase of the tram project encompasses 19 stops and serves a large part of the city. The original city tramway was 9.5 km long and is extended in the second phase along 8.5 km to a new terminus in the town of Denain. An old rail road has been used for this extension. A network of 'feeder' bus lines supports the regional coverage of the tramway. A completely new line opened in December 2013. This tramway is mainly single track and runs in a northern direction to Vieux-Condé.

The Bus: An Alternative to the Tram in Groningen (Netherlands)

Bus stop at Zernike served by buses of Q-link.

The office of the regional transport authority (*OV Bureau Groningen Drenthe*) came up with a bus alternative after the Groningen tram project had been called off. A new network was designed and branded *Q-link*. It runs at high frequency and has a larger capacity, thus enabling direct connections (so without changing) with economically important destinations in both the city

Continued

The Bus: An Alternative to the Tram in Groningen (Netherlands)—cont'd

and the region. *Q-link* buses run directly from regional towns to the University Medical Centre UMCG, the station and its immediate surroundings, the Zernike Campus, the Martini Hospital, the Europapark neighbourhood, and the station with the same name. Buses on the *Q-link* network call at five park and ride locations around the city. In order to make the creation of *Q-link* possible, investments were made in new, comfortable and environmentally friendly vehicles and infrastructure, amongst other things to enable operation with double-articulated buses.

In this way *Q-link* is an alternative for *RegioTram*, which had also been supposed to provide direct connections between the city and the region. The majority of transport to Zernike is processed by a direct *Q-link* shuttle line that goes around the city centre via the Westelijke Ringweg ('Western Ring Road'). Though the first phase of the tram project involved one line via the city centre and one line via the UMCG, the bus alternative provides two lines. Each line calls at two of the four main P + R locations. A third line is operated using new double-articulated buses and goes to the Zernike Campus via the city centre. Some of the buses continue to Zuidhorn after having passed Zernike.

Line 1 and 2 are operated with electric buses since December 10, 2017. *(Image by Patrick Ruiter (OV Bureau Groningen-Drenthe).)*

During 2017 substantial improvement took place when new lines and services were added. It was also decided to prepare the electrification of Line 1

The Bus: An Alternative to the Tram in Groningen (Netherlands)—cont'd

(according with the former tramway alignment), including a new Line 2 that offers a direct connection between the university and the regional Europapark station.

Q-link |

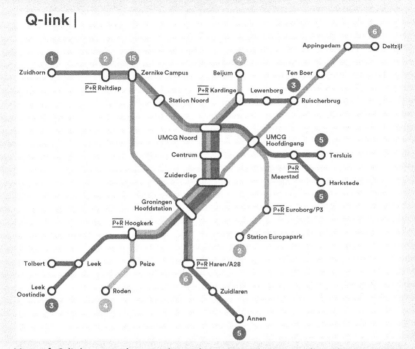

Map of Q-link network according plan 2017. The *green lines* (grey in print version) (1 and 2) represent in fact an extended and elaborated version of the originally proposed tramway. *(Map by OV Bureau Groningen-Drenthe.)*

Pragmatic Lessons From Olsztyn (Poland)

Contrary to the Groningen *RegioTram* the tramway project in Olsztyn has been successful, at least eventually. This is our 'mirror-case' to grab the necessary pragmatics of tramway projects. Additionally, Olsztyn allowed us a better understanding of the tragic planning and tender process in Groningen.

Continued

Pragmatic Lessons From Olsztyn (Poland)—cont'd

Tramway Olsztyn. The new trams are built by the Polish manufacturer Solaris. *(Image by MOs810.)*

Like Groningen in the Netherlands, the city of Olsztyn in Poland became very serious with their tramway project in 2010, when they launched a tender, and a year later when they awarded a design and construct contract (D&C) for a three-line system (11.5 km). And, like Groningen, this Polish city chose a non-classic contract, though their D&C was far less complicated than the DMFMO for Groningen (for a two-line system of 11.7 km, also tendered in 2010).

Map of the Olsztyn tramway network. Purple (black in print version) represents the new tramway (*narrow line* indicate single track branches), green (grey in print version) represents the former tramway (closed in 1965). *(Map by Jkan997.)*

Pragmatic Lessons From Olsztyn (Poland)—cont'd

However, while Groningen ended up in a complicated contract formation process (2011–12), Olsztyn commenced construction in 2011 short after the Spanish firm FCC got a contract of 62.5 million euros. Unfortunately, the relationship between this construction company and the assigning authority soon deteriorated. In August 2013, after several months of worsening co-operation, the contract was officially terminated. However, in contrast to Groningen, this didn't mean the end of the project. Olsztyn didn't want to waste the money that had already been invested, nor jeopardize their EU funding (as Groningen did). Hence, they decided to retender and to remove the design component from the new, now classic contract. Moreover, they concluded that it was necessary to split the new contract into six independently tendered contracts. This pragmatic approach turned out to be successful.

Moreover, by separating the design from the tramway construction tender, the city authorities created greater flexibility for themselves. For instance, they could reconsider the design task in the city centre for enhanced improvement of the public realm and usages by pedestrians and cyclists. It was hard work for them, because the approach required a lot of additional work for reviewed contract formation and related interface management. The reward however was there when, on 19 December 2015, the system officially opened. During the first few weeks the operation patterns and traffic management system required adaptations. The journey times had to be slightly increased. Again it was hard, though successful, work.

There was a most important lesson from this case: in many circumstances complicated tramway projects should be split up, particularly in the tendering and construction stages, and as Olsztyn proved, even in the stage of operation. An open, flexible approach is unavoidable to review planning, design, tendering, construction and operation when necessary.

7.3 REASONS FOR FAILURES AND RISKS

Based on our research into the Groningen *RegioTram*, The Hague *RandstadRail* and Utrecht *Uithof line* cases, we are able to list the causes for risks and failures of these kinds of projects. The results of a separate study into integrated contracts, like the DBFMO (Design, Build, Finance, Maintain, Operate) that was opted for in Groningen, have been taken into account.

Usually traditional risk management is conducted for each complicated public transport project and the Groningen *RegioTram* was no exception to this. Our checklist has therefore been based on an extensive study into the files of this project. The complex and sometimes overlapping factors have been summarized by us, thus creating a 10-point checklist. It is remarkable how the three projects differ from each other just when considering these points of traditional risk management.

1. Scope, content, interfaces, design/engineering;
2. Technology, safety;
3. Financing, business case;
4. Justification (ridership, economy, costs—benefits);
5. Political and executive decision-making;
6. Stakeholder commitment;
7. Residents' participation;
8. Planning and project organization;
9. Tender, contract;
10. Construction, operation.

Checklist of traditional factors for failures and risks to light rail projects (Van der Bijl, 2014):

1. The first point concerns scope, content and design. The organization of *RegioTram* did not approach this point very consistently, because its scope was increased more than once. In addition to this, it stands out that engineering is emphasized relatively early on in the design phase (even well before the scope statement phase). *RandstadRail* had suffered a lot from the interfaces between the numerous components of this hybrid system, which led to accidents and months of being out of service after it had opened. This first point on our checklist was approached most pragmatically in the *Uithof line* project (just as they approached most of these points). This project was split up; there was a separate tender for the substructure, which was ready by the time the tender for the permanent way arrived. The latter approach demands a lot of interface management.

2. The second point of technology and safety was given more attention in the *RandstadRail* project than in an average project and even played a role after operation had commenced. *RegioTram* never got to the complicated tram-train phase, but the specifications of the first city tram phase were still very complicated because of the necessary anticipation of the following regional phase within the domain of heavy rail.

3. The third point — financing and business case — justifies a chapter in its own right for all projects. As was stated before, the DBFMO contract used for *RegioTram* turned out to be a dead-end. *RandstadRail* was brought into being based on a traditional approach. The *Uithof line* in this respect consists of several subprojects, though the contribution by the national government had been achieved in a conventional way.

4. The justification of all three of these projects was mainly aimed at ridership; other arguments, as presented in Chapter 4, were only scarcely used. The initial societal cost–benefit analysis for the *Uithof line* was very limited. As was pointed out earlier, an adjusted analysis helped, because it took into account the important factor of reliability. No cost–benefit analysis had ever been done for *RegioTram*.

5. Political and executive decision making was thoroughly studied for the Groningen project. This classical point within risk management is the largest factor for failure of light rail projects, even larger than the point of justification, in spite of the non-traditional factors of risk and failure that will be discussed later. This major point largely explains how *RegioTram* failed, how *RandstadRail* was finally built after years of (non-)decision making, and how it was opportunistically decided to split up and construct the *Uithof line* in subprojects.

6/7. The next two points on the checklist, social inclusion of the project thanks to stakeholder commitment and residents' participation, played an important part in all three projects. Because of the location of *RegioTram* (mainly in the city centre) these points were relatively more important, thus contributing to the demise of this project.

8. Planning and project organizations have been challenging issues in each of the projects. The main conclusions are the following: *RandstadRail* has not benefitted from its double project organization, being one from The Hague and one from Rotterdam. Planning the *Uithof line* started well after a single, general project organization was founded in 2012. Before that moment the double organization (the municipality of Utrecht and the city region of Utrecht) was not sufficiently capable of getting things done. By the way, in 2008 it was already advised by Van der Bijl et al. to start a truly integral project organization. Its importance was confirmed by other consultants in the years following.

9/10. As stated before, tender/contract and construction/operation were approached unconventionally in the *RegioTram* project, using a DBFMO contract. Compared to this, *RandstadRail* was realized very traditionally in this respect. The same goes for construction and operation. As stated before, the *Uithof line* consists of several subprojects, but the contracts used are traditional; 'design and construct' was only applied to the substructure. Operating the *Uithof line* is a project in its own right. A purpose-founded tram company will provide management, maintenance and operation of the entire future tram system in the urban region of Utrecht (2018 and later years). This includes the existing line to Nieuwegein and later extensions.

Managing and controlling traditional factors of failure and risk is a basic condition for every successful project, but it is not enough. Our research into the 61 light rail cases in this book has brought forth three non-traditional factors. The first serious risk factor is what we would like to call the 'technocratic attitude' displayed by both decision makers (in politics, on executive levels, and amongst civil servants) and by those who work in the project organization (the head of the organization and their employees). They do not properly manage professionals and agents carrying out the assignment (the wrong questions that result in the wrong answers), either consciously or not, and aim overly at management and engineering. As a result and without wanting to, they are unable to deal with all stakeholders empathetically, in particular with some residents and politicians.

The second non-traditional risk is the attitude that comes with the assumption that the planning process is seen as a rational process. This attitude makes it difficult to really grasp the social dynamic that surrounds the project and act accordingly. Irrational behaviour displayed by stakeholders, action groups and other people involved is a normal part of every decision-making process. A naïve and technocratic approach in this context is one of the greatest risks for any light rail project.

Finally, tightly fencing off the project is likely to form a large risk to the project. It is true that the scope of the project has to be defined precisely and restrictedly, but on the other hand the contents and context should be approached as openly as possible. Projects are doomed to fail time after time when, as the project progresses in development, little to no attention is paid to the changing social, spatial and temporary characteristics.

The question is: how should factors of risk and factors of failure be dealt with? Our cases help lessons to be drawn for an improved approach to light rail projects and other projects on high-quality public transport. A general lesson is to first address the 'why' of the project, instead of focusing too quickly and to restrictedly on 'how' the project has to be tackled and 'what' exactly needs to be done. The traditional approach includes solely or mostly the latter. This was the case for the majority of our 61 cases. Consequently, the overall argumentation is insufficiently taken into consideration. The lesson learnt is to explore, emphasize and communicate the 'why' of a project using the five essential domains:

Effective mobility (E1) — effectiveness of transport and mobility.

Efficient city (E2) — efficiency and suitability of spatial use and spatial/urban (re)development.

Economy (E3) — prosperity and wellbeing in/for cities.

Environment (E4) — decreasing carbon footprints; sustainable cities.

Equity (E5) — socially inclusive cities.

Secondly, project management should accept and apply some sort of step-by-step planning. In the majority of the projects we studied project management had used rational planning, which applied especially to projects that included a complicated and integrated contract form. DBFMO projects are characterized by a technocratic belief in rational planning more than any other type of project. These DBFMO projects are the ones to be hit by unreliable practice that has to be evaluated every now and again. They either fail, like *RegioTram* Groningen, or smartly choose a reboot with a simpler, usually more traditional approach, like the Stockholm *Spårväg City*, or plod on if the legal limitations allow for that to happen. Even established projects can be haunted by their semirational pasts; the (integrated) contract may be reopened, like in our London/Croydon case, or all possible effort put into preventing bankruptcy, like in the Reims tram project.

Thirdly, there is a lesson to be learnt from project conceptualization in which the scope of the project is limited as much as possible. Similarly, use should be made of as many proven technologies as possible. When handling the surroundings of the project a broad view is required and the actual project should be made as small as possible. This way a smaller (initial) project can be implemented sooner and more reliably than relatively large projects. The main point is to create done deals; when something is built and already used it is considerably more difficult to end the project in the next phase. It is difficult to match this approach to the use of complex and long-term contracts. In connection to this the difference in approach between the Groningen *RegioTram* and the Utrecht *Uithof line* is evident.

The former was marked by an 'all-or-nothing' approach, whereas the latter was developed gradually and in a series of step-by-step developed subprojects.

Fourthly and finally, while the initial project, subproject or 'first phase' should opportunistically be as small and limited in scope as possible, the spatial and public surroundings require an as all-encompassing an approach as possible. This lesson implies socially engaged project management, opportunistic stakeholder management, and in particular an unconventional approach towards politics and government.

Investigations Into Ways of Tendering and Contracts

Our case Almaty (Kazakhstan) closed its traditional Sovjet-Union-style tramway in 2015, when a new light rail project was envisaged. Despite the fact that the proposed light rail will incorporate sections of the old tramway, a completely new Design, Build, Finance, Maintain and Operate (DBFMO) scheme has been developed. This case shows the apparent strong forces behind considerations for complicated tendering and organization of light rail projects.

The *RegioTram* project in Groningen was the first of its kind in the Netherlands. DBFMO implies that designing and building are concentrated at one party. The passage from design to construction is a sort of black box for the tendering party. The contractor fully optimizes the turnover of the specifications into a design and a construction plan, including management and maintenance. The financial component may be modest or substantial.

The former project agency of Groningen *RegioTram* has conducted a survey of examples of projects with these or similar contractual forms by 2010. The results of this research have been adapted since then and are summarized here. The selection and assessment of the projects was based on desk research, fieldwork and, in particular, through contacts with local stakeholders.

Contract Forms

DBFMO-Plus: Design Built, Finance, Maintain and Operate, including light rail vehicles.

DBFMO: Design Built, Finance, Maintain and Operate.

DBFM: ditto, but without operation (e.g., remains at existing operator).

DBM: ditto, but without financial component (moreover, size of the 'F' can vary).

DBMO: ditto, but with Operate component.

D&C: Design and Construct, mostly for infrastructure's basement and overhead catenary.

BOT: Built, Operate and Transfer, that is, after construction the system is operated for a short period by the winner of the tender (not more than 1–6 years) and then transferred to the client.

Investigations Into Ways of Tendering and Contracts—cont'd

PFI: Private Finance Initiative, means financing of the involved project by a private sector party.

Classic FD contract: Final design is the basis for the construction estimate and call for tender.

In this series more cases must be mentioned. First, our case of London/Croydon, where the 99-year (!) PFI contract for DBMO, signed in 1996 with private commercial operator Tramtrack Croydon Limited (TCL), was revised when, in 2008, TCL was acquired by Transport for London (TfL) and thus all the financial risks came back to the government at a high price.

Second, a recently added case of an integrated contract is the Liège (Belgium) tram project. Initially, this new tramway was due to open in 2017. The idea was to realize the project on the basis of a DBFM contract. Without the 'O', because the operator of all local and regional public transport throughout Wallonia, the French-speaking part of Belgium, is TEC ('Transport En Commun'). However, the project was seriously delayed due to violation of the financial requirements of the European Commission. Meanwhile, the Wallonian government has started a re-tender on basis of an adapted DBFM contract. Time will tell whether this project becomes a reality. The same goes for the ambitious project in Almaty. Neither in Liège nor in Almaty is a fast implementation very likely.

The realization of a tram project is extremely complex, regardless of the method of tendering: in the classical manner on the basis of a classic contract, or in the form of an integrated contract, such as DBFMO. Reference projects can then be helpful — not so much to be copied, but to get a better overview and to test and compare solutions.

The selection of cases here is based on three criteria. First, the characteristics of the project (a new tram system, or an extension of an existing network; the specific city or region). Second, the environment of the project (for example, urban or suburban) and third, the organization of the project (classic contract or integrated tendering, integral design or subdesign). For the purposes of this book, we mainly choose projects with an integral contract form, but some classic projects have been added for comparison.

Project: Antwerp, Deurne-Wijnegem (*Pegasus, Brabo I*)

Characteristics: Extension of current tram network in the region of Antwerp (Belgium), including some mixed traffic segments and two depots.

Contract: 'Design Build Finance Maintain' concerning tram infrastructure and non-tram infrastructure (urban space), respectively. No operations included, since *De Lijn* is the preferred operator for all urban and regional public transport in Flanders. No rolling stock included neither (lease was considered originally).

Continued

Investigations Into Ways of Tendering and Contracts—cont'd

Value: 147 million euros (excluding two separate contracts with regard to the depots).

Assessment: The project illustrated the new policy making in Flanders concerning alternative governmental investments very well. The project was successfully finished in 2012.

Project: Edinburgh Tram

Characteristics: New urban tramway connecting the airport to the waterfront via the inner city (Princes Street).

Contract: 'Design Build Maintain' concerning tram infrastructure.

Value: Originally 512 million pounds (during the first years it increased to 600 and 770 million pounds, and eventually to 1 billion pounds).

Assessment: Construction works started in 2009, but were quickly put to a stop due to several conflicts between the client (Transport Initiatives Edinburgh (TIE, 100% owned by the city) and a private consortium including the engineering company Bilfinger Berger).

During the summer of 2011, the project was almost cancelled completely, but after heavy debate in the city parliament it was decided to continue. The line configuration was reduced to the airport—city centre only (St Andrew Square, later extended to York Place). TIE was eliminated and the project management became the responsibility of a private company (Turner & Townsend). In this way, Edinburgh opened its tramway at May 31st in 2014, being much shorter than originally planned and even more expensive than planned (probably even more than 1 billion pounds).

Project: The Hague Region (*Line 19*)

Characteristics: *Line 19* is the new tangential line in the Hague region. It does not serve the city centre of The Hague, but connects residential areas to shopping centres and the city of Delft. The new tramway partly shares tracks with the existing tramway. The project was divided into two parts: 19A from Leidschendam to Delft and 19B from Delft to the University campus of Delft University of Technology.

Contract: The construction work of the tram infrastructure was tendered in a traditional way based on a final design. The operations are part of the current tram operations contract executed by HTM. Maintenance works will be part of the current contract between the transit authority (MRDH) and the operator (HTM). The rolling stock was tendered independent of this tramway by the transit authority.

Value: 130 million euros (excluding expected cost increase of part 19B).

Assessment: *Line 19* turned out to be a complicated project. Integration with the local environment (public space) had to be organized several times due to

Investigations Into Ways of Tendering and Contracts—cont'd

the amount of municipalities along the route. Line 19A was opened in 2010, but line 19B won't be in operation until 2020.

Project: Hasselt–Maastricht (*Spartacus, Phase 1*)

Characteristics: New regional tramway of 32 km, including a new urban route in Hasselt (Belgium) to the university (Diepenbeek). The tramway continues to the Dutch city of Maastricht over a former cargo railway and a new urban route. This tramway is planned as the start of a future regional light rail network.

Contract in Belgium (Flanders): Design, Build, Finance and Maintain with regard to the tram infrastructure. Operations are excluded since De Lijn will be the operator. An additional contract will be tendered regarding the fleet.

Contract in the Netherlands: Design and Construct (maintenance and operations will be executed by De Lijn).

Value: 243 million euros (estimation of the Flemish part, excluding fleet; excluding update of second version of the project)

Assessment: The opening was originally planned for 2015. Several issues however caused delay. Moreover, a revised version of the project was decided in 2016 when enforcement of the existing bridge over the river Maas in Maastricht turned out to be necessary. So far, the required additional funding has not been available, therefore it was decided to curtail the route and to create a terminus at the centre side of the river. The start of the project is now not foreseen until 2023, meaning that the total planning process will take over 20 years.

Project: Lyon (*Rhônexpress*, Part-Dieu–Saint-Exupéry; formerly 'Leslys')

Characteristics: Regional express tram from one of the main rail stations to the airport, sharing its route with an existing tramway (T3). These tracks were constructed some years before (being a reconstruction of a former heavy rail line). Some parts were newly constructed.

Contract: Design, Build, Finance, Maintain and Operate with regard to the tramway infrastructure and fleet.

Value: 110 million euros (consisting of 65 million euros with regard to the infrastructure).

Assessment: This is the first French project that was built and operated in this PPP way. The contract of 30 years was settled between the regional authority (*le Département du Rhône*) and a new consortium. In fact, it is a small project, consisting of newly built track 7 km outside the city. The project was finished in 2010.

Continued

Investigations Into Ways of Tendering and Contracts—cont'd

Project: Nice (*Ligne 1*)

Characteristics: Project of a new tramway in Nice connecting two suburbs via a route through the city centre. At two squares in the cities, no catenary is used (trams use their batteries at these sections). The integration of the tramway and urban space is very ambitious. An art project in the urban area was very important for this project. Moreover the project was combined with renewing the main sewer system in the city. '*Ligne 1*' is the first line of a new planned light rail network.

Contract: Traditionally organized. The authority CANCA (*Communauté d'Agglomération de Nice Côte d'Azur*) settled one contract with one construction company, based on a final design for public space and tram infrastructure. In addition, one contract was settled for the main workshop and the fleet was tendered. Operations were tendered as well and they are executed for 7 years by a consortium including Veolia.

Value: 560 million euros (including reconstruction of the main sewer system).

Assessment: Although several contracts were settled (e.g., workshop, fleet and operations), it is surprising that the construction works concerning the tramway infrastructure and public space are combined in one contract, meaning one client (CANCA) and one construction company. This was done deliberately, since in the opinion of the client the construction of the infrastructure is closely connected to the design of the public realm.

Project: Nottingham (*Nottingham Express Transit*, NET, Line 1/Line 2 and Line 3)

Characteristics: New urban tram system. Route via the city centre to the north of the agglomeration, partly using the former railway alignment. Line 1 heads to a park and ride facility. This new tramway was extended towards the south via a new bridge over the main train station with two branches (Line 2/3).

Contract: Line 1 — Design, Build, Finance, Maintain and Operate (27 years) concerning tram infrastructure and fleet, including PFI concession (30.5 years); Line 2/3 — Design, Build, Finance, Maintain and Operate (23 years), including maintenance and operations of the first line.

Value: Line 1 — 179 million pounds (PFI). Line 2/3 — 530.7 million pounds (PFI), plus 159.5 million pounds additional funding by the municipality, raised by urban parking revenues.

Assessment: Line 1 was opened in 2004; Line 2/3 in 2015. Both projects are considered a success. The amount of private prefunding with regard to Line 1 was relatively large.

The part of Line 2/3 with dedicated, independent tracks starting at the original terminal at the city side towards the other side of the railway station is

Investigations Into Ways of Tendering and Contracts—cont'd

not part of the DBFMO contract. This was chosen because they did not want to take the related risks (i.e., too late permit by Network Rail and potential higher costs).

Project: Reims (*Le tramway*)

Characteristics: New urban tramway in the city of Reims, applying an innovative traction system (APS) and reconstruction of the public space. Actually a restart of the failed project of 1991.

Contract: Design, Build, Finance, Maintain and Operate Plus; not only regarding the constructing, maintenance and operations of tramway infrastructure (fleet included), but also concerning operations of the tramway and all other urban public transport.

Value: 343 million euros.

Assessment: The trams designed by Alstom are tailormade to the region (famous due to its Champagne) due to the front part being shaped like a champagne glass. The tramway supports (re)structuring the city. Its presence stimulates urban (re)development at several places, for instance a new office district next to the new TGV station. This is a beautiful example of transit oriented development (TOD).

The consortium extended the original task. The APS part is extended and a new branch served by a second line to the new TGV station was introduced.

The total project was successfully finished in 2011, but in 2014 the operator Transdev faced financial problems. Due to a potential bankruptcy, negotiations of the 30-year contract were re-opened.

Project: Stockholm (*Spårväg City*)

Characteristics: New urban tramway connecting the main station, inner city and a popular park (Djurgården). The plan was to partly incorporate an existing tourist tramway (*Djurgårdslinjen*) serving the park and terminating at the border of the city centre.

Contract: Design, Build, Finance, Maintain and Operate regarding tramway infrastructure, including a 15-year concession.

Value: 2.5–3 billion SK (estimate).

Assessment: The project served by the DBFMO contract was stopped in June 2009 after only a few months, due to lack of knowledge and experience with this kind of contract. This project is a classic example of a poor application of DBFMO contracts. A first stage of the tram project was however realized in 2010, but by traditional supervision of the authorities (being the regional authority (SL) and the municipality of Stockholm).

Continued

Investigations Into Ways of Tendering and Contracts—cont'd

Project: Tel Aviv Light Rail (*Red Line*)

Characteristics: Metro-style tramway, the '*Red Line*', as part of a future high-quality light rail network.

Contract: BOT regarding infrastructure (unknown concerning fleet).

Value: 2 billion euros (estimate).

Assessment: The tendering of the integrated contract, the biggest in Israel ever, failed in November 2009. The ministry confirmed that it was impossible to achieve a financial closure of the project.

A revised version of the project started in December 2010.

Project: Zuid-Holland (*RijnGouwelijn*, East and West)

Characteristics: Regional light rail project in the Netherlands, that aimed at connecting the cities of Gouda, Alphen and Leiden (Lammenschans) via an existing heavy railway track and extending this connection via a new tramway through the city centre of Leiden to the coast (Katwijk and Noordwijk). This *RijnGouwelijn* (RGL) combined characteristics of an urban tramway (in Leiden) with a regional tramway at the east side of Leiden (track sharing with heavy rail trains between Leiden-Lammenschans and Gouda) and at the west side of Leiden a new dedicated tramway to the coast.

Contract: Regarding the newly built part the joint final design was the contract basis for tramway infrastructure and public space. In addition to that, several parts were gathered in subcontracts of the 'engineering and construct' type. Operations and fleet would have been combined in one contract.

Value: 310 million euros (east); 212 million euros (west).

Assessment: The tendering process was mainly traditionally executed, namely the selection of a construction company based on a final design. Some elements, however, were excluded and became part of the 'engineering and construct' contracts. Typically regarding the urban part, both infrastructure and public space were connected in one contract. The main reason for this choice was the risk with regard to the adjacent public space of the project. Normally, a contract would be closed as late as possible, to reduce these risks. They considered no other options for dealing with these risks. Finally, this is clearly no showcase for an integrated contract.

Although finally the processes with regard to the contracts went well, the project suffered from the start from slow political and governmental decision making and lack of societal approval. These were the main reasons for the project stopping in 2012 through lack of political support.

Conclusions

When an integrated contract is chosen, the method of how the distinction between the tramway infrastructure and the public space planning is settled is very important. Concerning the new tramway, Deurne-Wijnegem in Antwerp

Investigations Into Ways of Tendering and Contracts—cont'd

(Belgium), two separated contracts regarding tramway infrastructure and public space planning, respectively, were set. However, in Edinburgh (UK), improving public space while constructing the tramway was not considered at all, while the construction did cause a nuisance factor for shops and visitors.

The Edinburgh (UK) tram project lacked any ambition to combine the introduction of the tramway with enhancing public space. The nuisance proved to be a problem for shops and visitors. In the tramway *Line 19* project in The Hague area (the Netherlands), public space was not a substantial part of the classic contract. This area was the responsibility of the respective municipality. In Hasselt (Belgium) the topic of public space and tramway construction was partly managed outside the contract. The major part of the route uses former heavy railway alignments which means that integration with public space is not a major issue. In Maastricht (the Netherlands), an integrated contact was designed and the technical infrastructure was managed via a Design and Construct contract. The *Rhônexpress* in the (urban) area of Lyon (France) is a new tramway in a relatively open space; integration of tram and public space did not play a major role except for the entrance to the airport area. In Nice (France), the challenge of co-ordinating the public realm and tramway infrastructure was tackled by having one (public) entity being responsible for the total project, consisting of one main assignment, based on one final design (completed by some subprojects).

The ambitions regarding public space for the urban part of both tramway projects in Nottingham (UK) were set too low. In Stockholm (Sweden) however, exactly this issue caused the failure of the project. Integrating the tramway infrastructure was not possible (on time) and could thus not be managed in the planned contract (on time). In the light rail project in Tel Aviv (Israel) however, this challenge did not play a major role at all, since the main part of the route was by tunnel. Integration of surface sections of the route was modest and without any ambition. Finally, in the project of the *RijnGouwelijn* in the Leiden region (the Netherlands), the challenge of co-ordination in the urban part of the route was managed by letting the client closely co-operate with the municipality of Leiden based on one final design (completed by some subprojects).

In the case of integrated contracts, the level of integration of tramway infrastructure and public space is often limited. If the adjacent area and public space are a very important challenge anyway, these will be managed outside the contract. In Antwerp (Belgium), a separated contract on the public realm was settled in a Design, Build and Maintain format. In Lyon (France) the scope of the project and its contract only focused on the route in an open area outside the city so integration was not taken into account.

Groningen (Netherlands) set two separated documents, namely a final design regarding the public space and a functional set of requirements (being a

Continued

Investigations Into Ways of Tendering and Contracts—cont'd

specification of the expected output) in addition to the draft design of the tramway infrastructure.

If public space is actually an important part of the total challenge, the chosen contract is usually a traditional one. Nice (France) is a representative example. Making one party responsible for the total project (consisting of the tram infrastructure, public space, etc.) seemed successful, independent of splitting the total challenge into several (sub)contracts. If one entity is responsible for the tramway infrastructure and another entity is responsible for the public space, then co-ordination requires negotiating and co-operation. The experiences have shown that this often leads to poor co-ordination between public realm planning/design and tramway infrastructure planning/design, illustrated, for instance, by the case of *Line 19* in The Hague region (Netherlands).

Our main case of *RegioTram* Groningen (Netherlands) faced a typical co-ordination challenge, namely that of the final design of the public space and the functional requirements of the tramway infrastructure. This complicated the project greatly.

If a Design, Build, Finance, Maintain and Operate contract is settled for in an urban area, especially if it concerns a complex public space, the risk of delays is substantial, for instance due to legal procedures (e.g., Edinburgh), or even the risk of a total cancellation (e.g., Stockholm).

The Groningen case unfortunately illustrates an example where the co-ordination of the final design of public space and the functional requirements of the tramway infrastructure was not a success. Evaluating the process, it was not possible to adequately tackle uncertainties and unexpected events related to the public space. In addition, potential (unexpected) conflicts between the optimization of the tramway infrastructure on the one hand, and the optimization of the public realm on the other hand turned out to be unmanageable.

In addition to public space, other components of tramway projects also seem to be managed in separate contracts, such as depots (Antwerp) or specific civil constructions, for instance the bridge over the main railway in Nottingham.

The fleet is often managed outside the contract for the tramway infrastructure (e.g., in Antwerp, Hasselt and Edinburgh). In Edinburgh, for instance, the contract concerning vehicles and operations was settled first, hence, before managing a Design, Build and Maintain contract for construction of the tramway infrastructure. Sometimes, attempts were made to lease the fleet (Antwerp), but this proved to be very difficult. In Groningen, the intention was to let the decision on the fleet be part of the consultation of private parties. It was after this consultation that the final choice concerning fleet purchase was made.

Since the start of the economic crisis in 2008, private parties seem to be less willing to take large risks and are less reluctant to co-operate (Tel Aviv).

Investigations Into Ways of Tendering and Contracts—cont'd

Accordingly, in Nottingham (*Lines 2* and *3*) and in Groningen (*RegioTram*) only two consortia were interested in joining the final tender. Changes to the scope during the process endanger the success of an integrated contract (or its preparation) as in Stockholm for instance.

In our investigation Groningen, Reims, Nottingham (*Line 1*) and Liège are the only projects in which the Design, Build, Finance, Maintain and Operate contract and process completely covered the full project. And what were the results? Groningen failed. Reims succeeded but suffered severe financial issues after a few years. Nottingham succeeded and even extended the project. The tramway project of Liège faced substantial delays, since the contract had to be revised.

Lessons

The main lesson to be learnt from the above analysis of reference project cases is that the main challenge to a tramway project (such as Groningen) concerns the organization of the synergy between tramway infrastructure and public space. Related to this some specific lessons will be described.

The planned synergy can be achieved by set tramway infrastructure and public space under the responsibility of authority or client, where this authority uses an integrated plan for both aspects. Nice is a classic example of this approach. Other possibilities also exist, for instance setting up separate plans but all under the responsibility of the same client or authority. This is the method applied to some extent in Edinburgh. Another option is full separation of plans, hence, of responsibility of each domain and project. This implies solving all interface challenges by means of co-operation. This approach was applied in Leiden (*RijnGouwelijn*). This approach is also often applied in traditional tramway projects and contracts.

Some More Lessons

- Excellent cooperation between client or project organization and the municipality is a key condition for success of the project.
- An integrated contract could be applied in urban areas (as in Edinburgh), but if the part concerning public space becomes too ambitious, it requires specific attention to the co-ordination of the tramway infrastructure and public space.
- Integrated contracts do not necessarily consist of all components. Only Design, Build and Maintain could, for instance, also be effective (Edinburgh). But still, co-ordination with public space design (with or without separate tendering for reconstruction) remains a major challenge.
- It is not required that the fleet is part of the (integrated) contract. Antwerp and Edinburgh, for instance, show other possibilities.

Continued

Investigations Into Ways of Tendering and Contracts—cont'd

- If the size and contents of the contract are settled, the scope should not be changed subsequently. Changes to the scope endanger the success of the project, as shown by the Stockholm case. This implies that the preparation of the actual tendering is extremely important.
- In general, it is a risk to make private parties responsible for the financial risks of the project (as in Tel Aviv). This implies that during the preparation of the tendering the size of these risks should be minimized.
- It is apparent that a Design, Build, Finance, Maintain and Operate Plus contract (as in Groningen) is not suited well for this kind of relatively small, but complex, tramway projects. The complexity would have been reduced substantially if operations and the fleet were not part of the integrated contract. In addition, the legal, rigid, approach prevented a (re)start of the project.

CHAPTER 8

Investing in the City

Stockholm has developed a smart city-strategy. The Stockholmers needs, interests and opportunities are taken seriously in this regard, particularly the urban transport challenge. Light rail contributes to this strategy.

When considering our collection of 61 cases, the only conclusion we can draw is that it is necessary to invest in public facilities and infrastructure to ensure the future of cities. In conclusion we will therefore restate the arguments in favour of light rail and the reasons why light rail is important. We will return once more to the matter of assessment of light rail based on the 61 cases in this book. For a general conclusion we will focus on the phenomenon of the *Smart City*, which offers a suitable framework in which investments in light rail and in the city can be assessed based on their merits.

8.1 WHY LIGHT RAIL?

Our extensive argumentation in the previous chapters underlines the effectiveness and efficiency of light rail, as well as the value of this public facility to the economy, the environment and social inclusion. Our research and that by colleagues like Carmen Hass-Klau, Knowles and Ferbrache, which we are grateful to have made use of, prove the importance of light rail in an urban context. We would also like to stress that the arguments

Light Rail Transit Systems
ISBN 978-0-12-814784-9
https://doi.org/10.1016/B978-0-12-814784-9.00008-6

presented also apply to other forms of high-quality and sustainable transport. It can be put even more generally: the arguments presented apply to essential public investments in cities and the infrastructure and facilities that go with them.

To conclude, we will state our arguments again. Firstly, light rail can be used as an effective method of public transport. Assuming there is sufficient transport demand and a bandwidth that justifies light rail, this mode of transports enables cost-efficient operation. In addition, it turns out that the reliability of light rail operation not only contributes to cost-effectiveness, but also to the user value of the customers, because of the comfort and speed, and also because of the reliability provided by this mode of transport. This is why the argument of reliability deserves to be prioritized in societal cost−benefit analyses (SCBAs) more than it is the case currently. This goes for new projects, but also for changes and improvements to existing public transport.

Furthermore, rail-bound public transport, like light rail, turns out to be a powerful tool not only for urban planning and urban design, but also for mobility planning and traffic design. The post-war generation of new tramway systems (in France, for instance) and urban−regional light rail systems (for example in the US) have notably improved the quality of cities and urban regions, both in terms of space and mobility. This not only concerns aesthetic improvement and urban embellishment, but also the functional and social enhancement of cities.

In other words: light rail helps improve city structures. It is the precondition for urban growth and (re)development, fighting unrestrained expansion, and stimulating social cohesion. In addition to this, light rail represents sustainable preconditions for realizing environmentally friendly cities and mobility. Since light rail is electrically powered it helps reduce particles, emissions and traffic-related noise pollution. Light rail and other forms of high-quality public transport contribute to a modal shift from private cars to collective transport, and thus to reducing the total amount of traffic and the total number of vehicle movements. This is how light rail boosts energy saving.

Finally, light rail is favourable for economic conditions and performance of cities and urban regions; good accessibility is essential for the economic performance of a city. Although there are no simple, causal correlations, there is no doubt light rail and other forms of high-quality public transport contribute to measures and investments that increase the economic value of the city. Even economic investments on the spot can be induced by reliable, comfortable, fast, and sustainable public transport like light rail.

8.2 ASSESSMENT OF LIGHT RAIL

It would be wonderful if all the advantages of light rail described in this book could be expressed in measurable terms, but this is not always the case. Though we have proved that reliability of public transport can be computed meticulously, other benefits cannot always be put into numbers in a similar way. The fact that a benefit cannot always be quantified does not mean that it is not of value; on the contrary.

In spite of this executives and decision makers understandably find measurability important, which is something we would like to address in our consideration of societal cost—benefit analyses. Perspective is key to this. Through this book we have tried to show that full assessment should be expressed in the complete width of the spectrum that goes from fundamentally quantitative to highly qualitative. Quantifiable variables in financial and economic contexts are not the only factors that matter in assessing a light rail product; qualitative considerations that can be argued properly and help improve the city in logistic, economic, social, and ecological ways are also important.

Every form of public transport naturally has to be justified using financial and technical criteria for the ridership required and for responsible operation costs. More than anything, high-quality public transport like light rail is an essential condition for a healthy city and a healthy urban region. This is a vital facility, which should, therefore, be assessed and valued as such. The necessity is widely recognized in many Western countries and especially in economically successful parts of Asia, where the importance of good public transport is recognized and accepted more widely than it is in some Western European countries. In connection to this, the Netherlands, as well as England and Scandinavian countries tend to exaggerate the financial aspect. We are convinced benefits of light rail should encompass more than merely cost efficiency, let alone cost reduction. The public need for good public transport is simply too important for that. Investing in light rail as a condition for (re)development of cities is therefore absolutely necessary when considering logistic, social, and ecological benefits.

8.3 REVIEW OF OUR 61 CASES

A regional tram from The Hague on its way to new town Zoetermeer is approaching the Leidschenveen station of *RandstadRail*. Here both The Hague lines (RR3 and RR4) share tracks with light rail line E from Rotterdam.

Our Dutch main case *RandstadRail* teaches us that the introduction of light rail can offer numerous opportunities for quality improvements, especially where reliability is concerned. This, however, takes effort. This main case shows that an integral and complete approach is necessary on all levels of planning. It is not one single measure, but a combination of tools that enables providing travellers with a reliable service. Reliability ought to be taken into consideration no later than during the design stage of the network, when planning both the infrastructure and operation timetable. A shift in mindset from focusing on vehicles that should arrive on time to travellers that should arrive on time is needed and *RandstadRail* shows that this is possible, which results in increasing traveller satisfaction and increasing numbers of travellers. *RandstadRail* has largely been successful in the way its infrastructure was spatially and functionally integrated. Urbanization had a head start and developed faster than the planning process of *RandstadRail* did, which has resulted in a backlog for transit oriented development (TOD) in the near future, but the *RandstadRail* stations and stops are still well imbedded in their surroundings. The parts in The Hague and Rotterdam are nothing less than an unlikely collection of inspiring ways to fit light rail into an urban environment. Unfortunately, hardly any justice was done to the argument for environment and equity. This mainly goes for the social aspect and the way a light rail system like *RandstadRail* is supposed to encourage social cohesion in the city and the urban region, which was a point that had not been properly addressed, as far as we know.

The research into our main case of the *Uithof line* also shows that light rail has the potential to make a giant leap forward in terms of reliability, which is an important benefit for both travellers and operators. Travellers spend less time travelling and they experience less uncertainty about their time of arrival. In addition, operation becomes cheaper and this is the reason why many light rail projects are aimed at this aspect. What is surprising is that it is not incorporated in important decision support systems, like traffic models and societal cost—benefit analyses. The *Uithof line* case shows that there are possibilities to do this. We have described a method to express the benefits of improved reliability in social terms and the effects are considerable. The expected reliability benefits of the *Uithof line* alone turned out be two-thirds of the total costs. If these benefits had not been made explicit, the cost—benefit ratio would not have exceeded 1, which would definitely have been the end of the project. Therefore, it is recommended to explicitly consider these benefits in other projects in order for a truthful picture about costs as well as benefits to be painted.

Embedding the *Uithof line* in the existing city turned out to be a daunting task, in spite of the fact that the largest part of the line goes around the city centre and not through it. The start of the line is at Utrecht Central Station, which is the most complicated station hub in the Netherlands, while the immediate surroundings of the station are equally problematical. Nonetheless, a high-quality and feasible plan for this part of the route was developed. On the other side of the tramway is the Uithof university campus, and this makes for another challenging area in which the *Uithof line* has to be included as a city tram. A good plan was made available for this, too. It should be noted that the environmental benefits brought about by turning the busy bus line to the campus into a tramway only played a minor role. The value of the *Uithof line* and possible future extensions may turn out to be more significant as the environmental interests of electric urban infrastructure will start playing a more prominent role. The same thing might happen to the argument of equity, which so far has been completely left out of the *Uithof line* planning history. In spite of all this, it is remarkable how much this Utrecht plan has developed compared with its predecessor which was shut down in 1995. The initial plan was to have the tram pass through the city centre and head to the university campus. This plan was completely aimed at the aspect of transport, even though a high-quality design had been made for urban imbedding, including design for high-quality public realm.

Reducing the use of light rail to mere matters of traffic and mobility is what tends to be done to the Dutch projects. It played an undeniable role in shutting down the Groningen *RegioTram* (our third main case) and the *RijnGouwelijn* (Leiden region). It is remarkable how in the latter project, but also another Dutch project like *Line 19* ('Line 19' The Hague Region), the tramway was seen rather as a threat than as an improvement to the environment. It was included in the Groningen tram project that trees were to be guaranteed to be included and the second phase of *Line 19* (in the city of Delft) was seen as a threat and not as an opportunity to the new park on the university campus. The innovations of the Dutch case Zwolle-Kampen failed because of tender-related problems, though this project could have functioned as an example for new approaches to urban infrastructure.

So what about the remainder of our collection of 61 cases? For these roughly the same thing goes as for the previous Dutch projects: primarily the aspect of transport was the one really taken into consideration. In particular many English projects were affected by the same problem. We cannot help but notice that a lot of prematurely ended projects from our German cases (Aachen (Aix-la-Chappelle), Kiel, and Hamburg) would have been better able at resisting criticism if they had been equipped with broad argumentation. The same goes for the plans in cases like Antwerp (Belgium), Dublin (Ireland), Edinburgh (UK), Paris (France), and Saarbrücken (Germany), the only difference being that the tramway projects in these cities were realized, albeit only partially or with great delay.

Re-think Athens (Greece), on the other hand, is an excellent example of an integral approach to space and mobility, including environmental, economic and social aspects. *Re-think Athens* includes plans for large-scale urban restructuring and part of this is to extend the existing tramway through the city centre. Unfortunately, it is too soon to determine whether the plan will actually be realized. This has happened to tram projects in some of our other cases, like Barcelona (Spain), Detroit (Michigan, US), and Nice (France), which we see as good examples of a comprehensive approach. This is why we are curious to find out what will happen in Liège (Belgium). The tram project there was modelled after a French example and, after an initial, failed attempt, a new tender was put out in an integrated, Anglo-Saxon style. It remains to be seen how much this project can learn from the project in Reims (France), another case in our collection, where the same thing happened. TOD is a characteristic of all those projects and plans in which an above-average importance is attributed to urban context and (re)development. Concerning this we relied heavily on our double Los Angeles case, in which the historic (*Pacific Electric*) and the current (*Metro*) light rail systems, as well as their numerous overlaps, have been compared. This case shows very clearly why urban development and light rail are historically and presently linked to each other. This was confirmed in other cases, like Casablanca (Morocco), Edmonton (Alberta, Canada), Manchester (UK), Portland (Oregon, US), Sydney (Australia), Toyama (Japan), and Valenciennes (France), which greatly reaffirmed our faith in the importance of TOD and the role of light rail as a catalyst for urban (re)development.

8.4 SMART CITY

Light rail represents public conditions of cities that are healthy and safe and where social cohesion is promoted, partly because public places and facilities are widely accessible, like the new waterfront with its tramway in Kaohsiung, Taiwan.

The term 'Smart City' is often used to refer to cities whose facilities and complementary networks are created using digital information and digital communication technologies. It goes without saying that ICT can offer support in the realization and use of proper public transport, which is also recognized in this book. We will not deny that in this way ICT can contribute to the reduction of emissions and to more efficient use of resources, but to us Smart Cities are more than just places where smart technologies are applied. In the first place, it is not just about the technology (for instance light rail), but about the way the technology is used and applied, hence, sustainably and socially is embedded in society. In connection to this, light rail does not represent a transport technology, but instead it represents public conditions of cities that are healthy and safe and where social cohesion is promoted, partly because public places and facilities are widely accessible. Light rail as hard infrastructure contributes significantly to the necessary accessibility, but always in combination with soft and social infrastructure. The latter is what determines whether or not a light rail system turns out to be successful.

The history of the first generation of light rail in the early 20th century illustrates the necessary public inclusion of technology. These light rail systems, like the *Pacific Electric* in Los Angeles, would never have been implemented if they had not served the social and economic development of the city, nor if they had not done well commercially. Public transport systems in countries like the United States and France may have been prematurely discarded and disassembled in the mid-twentieth century. What can be said with certainty is that light rail was reintroduced in new forms in both countries nearly 25 years later. This time public considerations regarding a healthy residential environment played an important part, in addition to the economic and social considerations. American cities like Los Angeles wanted to reduce smog and car use, whereas France put more emphasis on liveable cities and city centres.

The success of light rail has been internationally recognized. Dozens of new light rail systems have been opened worldwide since the opening of the *Blue Line* in Los Angeles (California, US, 1990) and *Le Tramway* in Nantes (France, 1985). A lot of new projects have recently been concluded successfully outside Europe and North America. These projects are represented by our cases there, including Casablanca (Morocco), Dubai (UAE), Kaohsiung (Taiwan), Queensland (Australia), Rio de Janeiro (Brazil), and Zhuhai (China).

Again, Smart Cities are only truly sustainable if their infrastructures, networks and facilities (including light rail) are actually socially embedded. A light rail system is not successful until it is really safe, accessible and reliable. It needs to be experienced and recognized and, very importantly, it needs to be affordable to the intended users. Such social embedding is a crucial condition for successful implementation of a project. Unfortunately, we have come across quite a few light rail projects that have failed over recent years. The relatively high number of failures in England stands out in our collection of cases, while the Netherlands, too, has faced a considerable number of failures. These can be attributed to many reasons, both bad and good. Our main conclusion is that the absence of public foundations, combined with a technocratic approach to the project, should be indicated as being the main causes of failure. However, a Smart City is not a city where technology is offered, but a city where technology is publicly supported, valued and used. Only then will investments reach their true potential.

BIBLIOGRAPHY

REFERENCES

Van der Bijl, R.A.J., van Oort, N., September 2014. Light Rail Explained. Better Public Transport & More than Public Transport. European Metropolitan Transport Authorities, Paris.

Van Oort, N., van Nes, R., 2009a. Control of public transport operations to improve reliability: theory and practice. Transportation Research Record (2112), 70–76.

Van Oort, N., Brands, T., de Romph, E., Flores, J.A., 2015a. Unreliability effects in public transport modelling. International Journal of Transportation 3 (1), 113–130.

Van Oort, N., Sparing, D., Brands, T., Goverde, R.M.P., 2015b. Data driven improvements in public transport: the Dutch example. Public Transport 7 (3), 369–389.

Van Oort, N., van der Bijl, R.A.J., Roeske, R., 2015c. Success and failure aspects of light rail in the Netherlands. In: Transportation Research Board Annual Meeting, Washington.

Van Oort, N., 2011. Service Reliability and Urban Public Transport Design (T2011/2, TRAIL Ph.D. thesis Series, Delft). www.goudappel.nl/media/files/uploads/2011_Proefschrift_Niels_van_Oort.pdf.

Van Oort, N., 2016. Incorporating enhanced service reliability of public transport in cost-benefit analyses. Public Transport 8 (1), 143–160.

Vrije Universiteit, 1998. Hoe laat denk je thuis te zijn? Vrije Universiteit Vakgroep ruimtelijke economie, Centrum voor omgevings - en verkeerspsychologie, Amsterdam (In Dutch).

FURTHER READING

Annema, J.A., Koopmans, C., van Wee, B., 2007. Evaluating transport infrastructure investments: the Dutch experience with a standardized approach. Transport Reviews 27 (2), 125–150.

Arnold, L., 1997. Die Stadtbahn, die Stadt und ihre Bewohner. Der Nahverkehr (15), 45–54.

Axhausen, 2001. Searching for the rail bonus. European Journal of Transport and Infrastructure Research (1), 353–369.

Banham, R., 1971. The Architecture of Four Ecologies. Penguin Books, Los Angeles.

Bates, J., Polak, J., Jones, P., Cook, A., 2001. The valuation of reliability for personal travel. Transportation Research Part E 37, 191–229.

Ben Akiva, 2002. Comparing ridership attraction for rail and bus. Transport Policy (2), 107–116.

Bertaud, A., Poole, R., 2007. Density in Atlanta: Implications for Traffic and Transit. Reason Foundation Policy Brief 61.

Besseling, P., Groot, W., Verrips, A., 2004. Economische toets op de Nota Mobiliteit. CPB, Document 65, Den Haag (In Dutch).

Bradshaw, C., June 2004. The Green Transportation Hierarchy. A Guide for Personal and Public Decision-Making (Revised Version). Ottawa.

Brezina, T., 2011. Light Rail Systems Design. A Human Transport Planning Criteria Centered Approach — Applied to the City of Ljubljana. Vdm Verlag, Saarbrücken.

Bunschoten, T., Molin, E., van Nes, R., 2013. Tram or bus; does the tram bonus exist? In: European Transport Conference.

Cain, 2009. Quantifing the Importance of Image and Perception to Bus Rapid Transit, Report U.S. Department of Transport.

Cats, O., West, J., Eliasson, J., 2014. Appraisal of increased public transport capacity. In: Presented on the 3rd European Symposium on Quantitative Methods in Transportation Systems.

Cats, O., Yap, M., van Oort, N., 2016. Exposing the role of exposure: public transport network risk analysis. Transportation Research Part A: Policy and Practice 88, 1—14.

CERTU, 2005. Déplacements et commerces. Impacts du tramway sur le commerce dans différentes agglomérations françaises. CERTU, Lyon.

Cervero, R., 1998. The Transit Metropolis. A Global Inquiry. Island Press, Washington DC, Chicago.

Chowdhury, S., Chien, S., 2001. Dynamic vehicle dispatching at intermodal transfer station. In: Transportation Research Board 80th Annual Meeting, Washington, DC.

Currie, 2004. Demand performance of bus rapid transit. Journal of Public Transportation (8), 41—55.

Curtis, C., Renne, J.L., Bertolini, L. (Eds.), 2009. Transit Oriented Development. Making it Happen. Ashgate, Burlington, Farnham.

Davies Gleave, S., 2005. What Light Rail Can Do for Cities (London).

De Bruijn, H., Veeneman, W., 2009. Decision making in light rail. Transportation Research Part A 43, 349—359.

De Cea, J., Fernandez, E., 1993. Transit assignment for congested public transport systems: an equilibrium model. Transportation Science 27 (2), 133—147.

Demoro, H.W., 1989. Light Rail Transit on the West Coast. Quadrant Press, New York.

Eijgenraam, C.J.J., Koopmans, C.C., Tang, P.J.G., Verster, A.C.P., 2000. Deel I Hoofdrapport. Evaluatie van grote infrastructuurprojecten. Leidraad voor kosten-baten analyse. Onderzoeksprogramma economische effecten infrastructuur. Centraal Planbureau en Nederlands Economisch Instituut (In Dutch).

European Commission, 2011. White paper on Transport.

Flyvbjerg, B., February 2007. Cost overruns and demand shortfalls in urban rail and other infrastructure. Transportation Planning and Technology 30 (1), 9—30.

Frumin, M., Uniman, D., Wilson, N.H.M., Mishalani, R., Attanucci, J., 2009. Service quality measurement in urban rail networks with data from automated fare collection systems. In: Proceedings of CASPT Conference, Hong Kong.

Furth, P.G., Muller, T.H.J., 2006. Service reliability and hidden waiting time: insights from automated vehicle location data. Transportation Research Record: Journal of the Transportation Research Board 1995, 79—87.

Furth, P.G., Muller, T.H.J., 2009. Optimality conditions for public transport schedules with timepoint holding. Public Transport 1, 87—102.

Girnau, G., et al., 2000. Stadtbahnen in Deutschland/Light rail in Germany. Verband Deutscher Verkehrsunternehmen, Düsseldorf.

Haaglanden, S., 2003. Programma van Eisen RandstadRail (In Dutch).

Hall, P., 1982. Great Planning Disasters. University of California Press, Oakland, CA.

Hall, P., 2014. Good Cities, Better Lives. How Europe Discovered the Lost Art of Urbanism. Routledge, London, New York.

Hass-Klau, C., Crampton, G., 2002. Future of Urban Transport, Learning from Success and Weakness: Light Rail. Environmental and Transport Planning, Brighton.

Hass-Klau, C., Crampton, G., Weidauer, M., Deutch, V., 2000. Bus or Light Rail: Making the Right Choice. A Financial, Operational and Demand Comparison of Light Rail, Guided Buses, Busways and Bus Lanes. Environmental and Transport Planning, Brighton.

Hass-Klau, C., Crampton, G., Benjari, R., 2004. Economic Impact of Light Rail. The Results of 15 Urban Areas in France, Germany, UK and North America. Environmental and Transport Planning, Brighton.

Hatcher, C.K., Schwarzkopf, T., 1983. Edmonton's Electric Transit: The Story of Edmonton's Streetcars and Trolley Buses. Railfare Enterprises Ltd., Toronto, Canada.

Hensher, D.A., Rose, J.M., Collins, A., 2011. Identifying commuter preferences for existing modes and a proposed metro in Sydney, Australia. Public Transport: Planning and Operations 3 (2), 109−147.

Heuvelhof, T., et al., 2008. Het RandstadRail-project: Lightrail, Zware opgave. TU-Delft, Stadsgewest Haaglanden (In Dutch).

Hickman, M., 2004. Evaluating the benefits of bus automatic vehicle location (AVL) systems (Chapter 5). In: Levinson, D., Gillen, D. (Eds.), Assessing the Benefits and Costs of Intelligent Transportation Systems. Kluwer, Boston.

Hoogendoorn-Lanser, Bovy, 2005. Modelling route choice behaviour in multi-modal transport networks. Transportation 32, 341−368.

Husler, 1996. Strassenbahnprojekte in der Standardisierten Bewertung. Der Nahverkehr (14), 55−62.

Israeli, Y., Ceder, A., 1996. Public transportation assignment with passenger strategies for overlapping route choice. In: Lesort, J.B. (Ed.), Transportation and Traffic Theory. Elsevier Science, Amsterdam.

Jacobs, J., 1961. The death and life of great American cities. In: The Failure of Town Planning. Random House.

Johanssen, P.O., 1991. An Introduction to Modern Welfare Economics. Cambridge University Press, Cambridge.

Kanacilo, E.M., van Oort, N., 2008. Using a rail simulation library to assess impacts of transit network planning on operational quality. In: Allen, J., Arias, E., Brebbia, C.A., Goodman, C.J., Rumsey, A.F., Sciutto, G., Tomii, N. (Eds.), Computers in Railways XI. WIT Press, Southampton, UK, pp. 35−44.

Kapteijn, K., van Erp, T., van Susteren, A., van der Bijl, R.A.J., Veeneman, W., 2012. OV van de metropool Randstad en zijn stedelijke regio's in internationaal perspectief; Potentials and barriers for (new) public transport. NGI/APPM, Hoofddorp.

Kasch, V., 2002. Schienenbonus: Es bleiben Fragen. Der Nahverkehr (3), 39−43.

Knowles, R., Ferbrache, F., 2014. An Investigation into the Economic Impacts on Cities of Investment in Light Rail Systems'. UK Tram, Birmingham.

Knowles, R., Ferbrache, F., 2016. Evaluation of wider economic impacts of light rail investment on cities. Journal of Transport Geography 54, 430−439.

Laisney, F., 2011. Atlas du tramway dans les villes françaises. Éditions Recherches, Paris.

Lee, A., van Oort, N., van Nes, R., 2014. Service reliability in a network context. Transportation Research Record (2417), 18−26.

Lesley, L., 2011. Light Rail Developers' Handbook. J. Ross Publishing, Fort Lauderdale, Florida.

Li, Z., Hensher, D.A., Rose, J.M., 2010. Willingness to pay for travel time reliability in passenger transport: a review and some new empirical evidence. Transportation Research Part E 46, 384−403.

Li, Z., Hensher, D.A., Rose, J.M., 2013. Accommodating perceptual conditioning in the valuation of expected travel time savings for car and public transport. Research in Transportation Economics 39, 270−276.

Litman, 2010. Transportation Elasticities; How Prices and Other Factors Affect Travel Behaviour. Victory Transport Policy Institute.

Liu, R., Sinha, S., 2007. Modelling urban bus service and passenger reliability. In: Proceedings of Instr 2007 Conference, The Hague.

Mandri-Perrott, C., 2010. Private Sector Participation in Light Rail/Light Metro Transit Initiatives. The World Bank.

McDonald, F., 2000. The Construction of Dublin. Gandon Editions, Dublin.

Megel, 2001. Schienenbonus: Nur ein Mythos? Der Nahverkehr 19 (6), 20–23.

Mepham, D.N., 2013. Transitioning from transit oriented development to development oriented transit. In: A Case Study of the Gold Coast Light Rail Project. Bond University, Gold Coast, Queensland, Australia.

Mouter, N., Annema, J.A., van Wee, B., 2013. Attitudes towards the role of cost–benefit analysis in the decision-making process for spatial-infrastructure projects: a Dutch case study. Transportation Research Part A: Policy and Practice 58, 1–14.

Muller, T.H.J., Furth, P.G., 2000. Integrating bus service planning with analysis, operational control and performance monitoring. In: ITS 10th Conference Proceedings, Washington, DC.

Murray, D., 2015. Light Rail Infrastructure, second ed. Createspace Independent Pub.

Noland, R., Polak, J., 2002. Travel time variability: a review of theoretical and empirical issues. Transport Reviews 22, 39–54.

Noland, R., Small, K.A., 1995. Travel time uncertainty, departure time and the cost of the morning commute. In: Proceedings of 74th Annual Meeting of Transportation Research Board, Washington DC.

OECD/ITF, 2009. Improving Reliability on Surface Transport Networks.

O'Flaherty, C.A., Mangan, D.O., 1970. Bus passengers waiting time in central areas. Traffic Engineering Control 11, 419–421.

Peek, G.J., van Hagen, M., 2002. Creating synergy in and around stations: three strategies in and around stations. Transportation Research Record (1793), 1–6.

Pelletier, M., Trepanier, M., Morency, C., 2011. Smart card data use in public transit: a literature review. Transportation Research Part C: Emerging Technologies 19 (4), 557–568.

Priemus, H., Konings, R., 2001. Light rail in urban regions; what Dutch policymakers can learn from experiences in France, Germany and Japan. Journal of Transport Geography 9, 187–198.

RAND Europe, AVV, 2005. The Value of Reliability in Transport: Provisional Values for The Netherlands Based on Expert Opinion. Leiden/Rotterdam.

Rietveld, P., Rouwendal, J., Verhoef, E.T., 2000. Enkele welvaartseconomische aspecten van de evaluatie van grote infrastructuurprojecten. Tijdschrift Vervoerwetenschap 36, 34–40 (In Dutch).

Rietveld, P., Bruinsma, F.R., van Vuuren, D.J., 2001. Coping with unreliability in public transport chains: a case study for Netherlands. Transportation Research 35A, 539–559.

Savelberg, F., Bakker, P., 2010. Betrouwbaarheid en robuustheid op het spoor. Kennisinstituut voor Mobiliteitsbeleid, Den Haag (In Dutch).

Schmöcker, J.D., Bell, M.G.H., 2002. The PFE as a tool for robust multi-modal network planning. Traffic Engineering and Control 44 (3), 108–114.

Seddon, P.A., Day, M.P., 1974. Bus passengers waiting times in greater Manchester. Traffic Engineering Control 15, 422–445.

SHRP 2 Reliability Project L05, 2013. Incorporating reliability performance measures into the transportation planning programming processes. In: Transportation Research Board of the National Academies, Strategic Highway Research Program, Washington, DC.

Significance, VU University, John Bates Services, TNO, NEA, TNS NIPO, PanelClix, 2013. Values of Time and Reliability in Passenger and Freight Transport in The Netherlands, Report for the Ministry of Infrastructure and the Environment. Significance, The Hague.

Smith, J.J., Gihring, Th.A., 2010. Financing Transit Systems through Value Capture. An Annotated Bibliography. Victoria Transport Policy Institute, Victoria, British Columbia.

Snelder, M., Tavasszy, L.A., 2010. Quantifying the full reliability benefits of road network improvements. In: Proceedings of WCTR 2010, Lisbon, Portugal.

Tahmasseby, S., van Oort, N., van Nes, R., 2008. The role of infrastructure on public transport service reliability. In: Proceedings of the 1st International IEEE. Conference on Infrastructure Systems: Building Networks for a Brighter Future, pp. 1–5.

Tan, W., 2013. Pursuing Transit-Oriented Development. Implementation through Institutional Change, Learning and Innovation (Ph.D.). University of Amsterdam.

TRB, 1978. Glossary of Urban Public Transportation Terms. Transportation Research Board, Washington, DC.

Tseng, Y.Y., 2008. Valuation of Travel Time Reliability in Passenger Transport (Ph.D. thesis). Vrije Universiteit, Amsterdam.

Turnquist, M.A., Bowman, L.A., 1980. The effects of network structure on reliability of transit service. Transportation Research Part B 14, 79–86.

Van de Boomen, T., Venhoeven, T., 2012. Mobiele stad. Over de wisselwerking van stad, spoor en snelweg. NAI010 Uitgevers, Rotterdam (In Dutch).

Van der Bijl, R.A.J., September 1998. Leicht durch Stadt und Landschaft – light rail – a convenient means of regional and city transport. Topos 24, 23–31.

Van der Bijl, R.A.J., April 1999. Light rail in Nederland: goed nieuws, maar vooral slecht nieuws. Blauwe Kamer 42–47.

Van der Bijl, R.A.J., June 2000. Das große Umsteigen – the big transfer. Topos 31, 66–73.

Van der Bijl, R.A.J., 2003. In: Priemus, H., et al. (Eds.), Light rail en regionale planning. ICES, stad & infrastructuur, pp. 68–74 (In Dutch).

Van der Bijl, R.A.J., 2006. Portland: urban planning by streetcar. Scape 2, 8–81.

Van der Bijl, R.A.J., 2007a. TramTrain & RegioTram. In: Permanent Way Institution Conference, Amsterdam, October 2007.

Van der Bijl, R.A.J., May 2007b. RandstadRail. What went wrong? Tramways and Urban Transit 178–179.

Van der Bijl, R.A.J., Juni 2008. Gebiedsontwikkeling en openbaar vervoer. NAW Dossier. Bouwfonds Property Development (In Dutch).

Van der Bijl, R.A.J., 2009. Public transport and urban planning. In: Tekna Conference, Bergen, Norway, February 2009.

Van der Bijl, R.A.J., 2012. Sustainable city transport. A pragmatic view. In: EBC Sustainable Development Conference, Tokyo, April 2012.

Van der Bijl, R.A.J., 2013a. Beknopte geschiedenis. In: Tan, W., et al. (Eds.), Knooppuntontwikkeling in Nederland. (Hoe) moeten we Transit-oriented Development Implementeren? Platform31. Universiteit van Amsterdam, Vrije Universiteit, Amsterdam, pp. 25–36 (In Dutch).

Van der Bijl, R.A.J., 2013b. Another look at the case of Fukuoka. The 'quick wins' in urban mobility. In: Expert Meeting Fukuoka 2013. Moving from Concepts to Action, Fukuoka, Japan, June 2013, pp. 5–6.

Van der Bijl, R.A.J., 2014a. Transit oriented development. Basics & examples. In: Conference, Transit Oriented Development: Integration between Land Use and Sustainable Transport, Almaty Kazakhstan, October 2014.

Van der Bijl, R.A.J., October 2014b. Sustainable City Transport. A Pragmatic View for Kazakhstan. Al-Farabi Kazakh National University, Almaty Kazakhstan.

Van der Bijl, R.A.J., 2014c. T.O.D. for Aerotropolis. Essentials, cases, trends. In: International Forum on Managing Transit-Oriented Development, Taiwan, April 2014.

Van der Bijl, R.A.J., 2014d. Incremental light rail planning. Approaches and example. In: Sintropher Conference, Brussels, February 2014.

Van der Bijl, R.A.J., Février 2014e. Gare Centrale. Université de Liège, Faculté d'Architecture.

Van der Bijl, R.A.J., Bukman, B., August 2014. Re-think Athens. 'We hebben een magisch plan gemaakt'. Blauwe Kamer 36—41 (In Dutch).

Van der Bijl, R.A.J., de Zeeuw, F., Augustus 2009. Integratie openbaar vervoer in gebiedsontwikkeling. Openbaar Bestuur, pp. 2—7 (In Dutch).

Van der Bijl, R.A.J., Kuehn, A., 2004. Tramtrain: the 2nd generation. New criteria for the 'ideal tramtrain city'. In: Association for European Transport during Their European Transport Conference (ETC 2004), Strasbourg, October 2004.

Van der Bijl, R.A.J., et al., 2005. Development of Principles and Strategies for Introducing High Quality Public Transport in Medium Sized Cities and Regions (HITRANS). Best Practice Guides. HiTrans, Stavanger, Norway, pp. 1—5.
Note: various other authors and consultants did contribute to these five handbooks which were compiled under responsibility of the HiTrans international steering group.

Van der Bijl, R.A.J., Guinée, A., December 1993. Trams in Parijs. Opwaardering van Stad en Openbare Ruimte. Blauwe Kamer 17—23 (In Dutch).

Van der Bijl, R.A.J., Hendriks, M., Fabric, 2010. Station Centraal. Over het samenbinden van station en stad. 010 Publishers, Rotterdam (In Dutch).

Van der Krabben, E., et al., 2013. Onderzoek innovaties bij integrale gebiedsontwikkeling en knooppuntontwikkeling. VerDus/Radboud universiteit, Nijmegen (In Dutch).

Van Loon, R., Rietveld, P., Brons, M., 2011. Travel-time reliability impacts on railway passenger demand: a revealed preference analysis. Journal of Transport Geography 19 (4), 917—925.

Van Oort, N., 2009a. International Benchmark, Reliability Urban Public Transport, Summary Results. Report HTM and Delft University of Technology.

Van Oort, N., 2009b. Service reliability: a key factor. Public Transport International 16—18.

Van Oort, N., 2009c. On-time vehicles at RandstadRail. Public Transport International 18—19.

Van Oort, N., December 2014. Incorporating service reliability in public transport design and performance requirements: international survey results and recommendations. Research in Transportation Economics 48, 92—100.

Van Oort, N., van Nes, R., 2009b. Regularity analysis for optimizing urban transit network design. Public Transport 1 (2), 155—168.

Van Oort, N., Boterman, J.W., van Nes, R., 2012. The impact of scheduling on service reliability: trip-time determination and holding points in long-headway services. Public Transport 4 (1), 39—56.

Van Oort, N., Brands, T., de Romph, E., Yap, M., 2016. Ridership evaluation and prediction in public transport by processing smart card data: a Dutch approach and example (Chapter 11). In: Kurauchi, F., Schmöcker, J.D. (Eds.), Public Transport Planning with Smart Card Data. CRC Press.

Veeneman, W., 2011. Opties voor de lijn Kampen Zwolle; een advies voor de Provincie Overijssel. TU Delft (In Dutch).

Vuchic, V.R., 1999. Transport for Livable Cities. Center for Urban Policy Research, New Jersey.

Wilson, et al., 1992. Improving Service on the MBTA Green Line through Better Operations Control, Transportation Research Record 1361. TRB, National Research Council, Washington, DC, pp. 296—304.

INDEX

Note: 'Page numbers followed by "f" indicate figures, "t" indicate tables and "b" indicate boxes.'

Printed in the United States
By Bookmasters